And Now, a Word from Our Creator:

Russ Holloman, Ph.D.

WestBow
PRESS
A DIVISION OF THOMAS NELSON

WestBow Press books may be ordered through booksellers or by contacting:

WestBow Press
A Division of Thomas Nelson
1663 Liberty Drive
Bloomington, IN 47403
www.westbowpress.com
1-(866) 928-1240

Because of the dynamic nature of the Internet, any web addresses or links contained in this book may have changed since publication and may no longer be valid. The views expressed in this work are solely those of the author and do not necessarily reflect the views of the publisher, and the publisher hereby disclaims any responsibility for them.

Any people depicted in stock imagery provided by Thinkstock are models, and such images are being used for illustrative purposes only.

Certain stock imagery © Thinkstock.

ISBN: 978-1-4497-2643-0 (sc)
ISBN: 978-1-4497-2644-7 (hc)
ISBN: 978-1-4497-2642-3 (e)

Library of Congress Control Number: 2011916005

Printed in the United States of America

WestBow Press rev. date: 11/2/2011

In Memoriam

Lenora Strebeck Holloman

23 January 1929–1 September 2008

Lenora made everything beautiful with her smile and sunny disposition. Love, doing the right thing, and serving others were guideposts on her journey through life as she walked humbly with God.

Contents

Introduction

"In the beginning God . . . The grace of our Lord Jesus Christ be with you all. Amen." (Genesis 1:1 and Revelation 22:21)

These are the opening and closing words of God's story—a story of love, disobedience, forgiveness, and redemption. Theatrically speaking, it is a drama in three acts telling God's story of His relationships with His earthly family. Although the acts are consecutive each is open-ended and ongoing. They are still being played out today on the stages of heaven and earth.

In the first act God created the universe and all that is in it. In His creation He saw Himself; everything He created He judged to be good. The grandest part of His creation, however, was man—not because we are inherently good but, rather, because we were made in His own image and likeness for fellowship with Him. Unfortunately, the free will He gave us, which was necessary for true fellowship, was misused by Adam and Eve to disobey Him.

In the second act God provided a moral law or plan for us to live by. He pledged His continuing love for us and His desire to restore the fellowship that was broken in the Garden of Eden. As parts of a new covenant of forgiveness and redemption, He provided us a model (Jesus) of righteous living and rules (The Bible) to obey in our relationship with Him and with others here on earth.

Included in God's moral law are rules for right and wrong behavior and thinking. What is right He commanded; what is wrong He prohibited. The purpose of His moral law is to help us live righteous lives and to protect us from what is sinful, injurious, and corrupting. In each word of instruction God's wisdom and logic are evident. The effect of honesty, for example, is good; it is commanded. The effect of greed, on the other hand, is bad, it is prohibited.

This book is concerned with the third act, where we respond to God's moral law and embrace His plan for our lives. Our response is the telling of our own life's story. God wants it to be a story of love and joyful obedience. He wants us to know how much He loves us and how much He wants us to be his family.

Sixty-five of God's words of instruction are discussed from the perspective that each word is both good theology and good psychology. Included are both commandments and prohibitions, do's and don't's, shall's and shall not's. All the chosen words are important. Granted, some are seemingly more important than others in God's scheme of things. But I don't know whether this difference is simply a matter of degree or a larger difference of kind.

My thirty-plus years of university teaching were characterized by student-teacher dialogue—the give-and-take of classroom discussion. That is not possible here. Still, I have tried to keep you in mind as I wrote each sentence. I imagined your reactions, your comments, and your questions.

My professional training was in psychology with a strong emphasis on perception and cognition, disciplines which deal with how we interpret and give meaning to our physical, social, and spiritual experiences. With this background, I sought a balance of both theological and psychological understandings of each of God's words. I have no seminary training and there is no "Reverend" before my name. My right and my competence to write about these subjects might be questioned. You will have to decide that question for yourself. I ask only that you refrain from hasty judgments.

It has always bothered me that we complicate the telling of God's story. Something He wants all of us to know, understand, and obey should be told in the simplest terms possible. In spite of our difficulties in reading, hearing, and understanding God's story we still hunger for it, wishing it wasn't so hard to receive. Because of this, I have tried to write in a simple, straight-forward manner—hopefully with the easily understood language I used in telling Bible stories to my children.

Russ Holloman, Ph.D.
Evans, Georgia
2011

1

THE KINGDOM OF GOD

Some Pharisees asked Jesus when the Kingdom of God would come. His answer was:

> *"The Kingdom of God does not come in such a way as to be seen. No one will say, 'Look, here it is!' or, 'There it is!' because the Kingdom of God is within you."* Lk 17:20-21. (GNB)

Throughout the ages we have searched—for Camelot, for the Golden Fleece, for Utopia, for Eldorado, for the pot of gold at the end of the rainbow. Our search continues today with a new focus and a new sense of urgency. Whatever name we give to our search, it is an expression of our need to find meaning and purpose in our lives. It is a reflection of what Paul Tillich has called the ultimate concern in our lives: a religious concern.

A traditional definition of ultimate is that which comes last in our lives. For all of us that is death. An elderly woman in the nursing home where my mother lived for a while often shared this circumstance with me when she would say, "I'm just waiting until the Lord calls me home." It was her belief and expectation that when she died she would be welcomed by God into His kingdom. But another definition of ultimate—the one I like—is that which is most important to us. This definition suggests that the woman in the nursing home did not have to wait until she died to know God's Kingdom.

Why do we look to the future for something we can have today? Why are we always striving (for something) when we can arrive and claim it? Why are we always looking outside ourselves for something that is within us?

The "something" in each of the above questions is the Kingdom of God. The interpretation of Jesus' statement, "The Kingdom of God is within you." has not been universally accepted. Questions abound. Did Jesus mean the Kingdom of God was actually "within" the skeptical Pharisees who had asked the question about the Kingdom's coming? Or did he mean that the Kingdom of God is "among you? "Within you" is preferred by many translations of the Bible, both because of manuscript evidence and the fact that it logically leads to "among you." If translated "among you,", "within you" would not logically follow.

Whichever translation you prefer, it does seem that Jesus was referring to the Kingdom as an inward, spiritual state. It is something that works in our hearts producing new people, new relationships, and new understandings of the presence of God "within" us. It produces a new reality.

Recognizing the negative attitudes of the Pharisees and the fact that Jesus made his "within" statement to them does not detract from the plausibility of this interpretation. Jesus was reminding the Pharisees that they were looking for the Kingdom in the wrong place. Instead of welcoming it in their own hearts and making it become a reality for them, they were looking for external signs of a physical kingdom. What Jesus said to the Pharisees is applicable to us.

I'm not suggesting that a neurosurgeon can actually locate the Kingdom of God within us. It's not that way, just as astronauts can't locate Heaven. In our Bible, the terms Kingdom of God and Kingdom of Heaven are sometimes used interchangeably. The Bible tells us, too, that God is spirit. God's Kingdom must also be spirit for where God is there is His Kingdom.

Like the Pharisees, we want to think of God's Kingdom as a place, something with a form including streets, buildings, and, hopefully, golf courses. We are too linear, too pragmatic, too left-brained to accept Jesus' declaration that the Kingdom of God is within us. How can something with a form actually be inside us? The Kingdom of God is beyond form, it is spirit. Form dies, spirit lives.

The Kingdom of God is a condition of the heart—not something above the earth which we go to at death. Nor is it something we have to wait for. It has no yesterday and no tomorrow, yet it has both a present and future quality. It has come; it is still coming. It is realizable, but not yet fully realized. We can know the Kingdom of God today, not in its full glory, perhaps, but we can know the joy, the glory, and the abundant life that Christ promised.

We become conscious of the Kingdom of God when we live in right relationships with God and with each other. It is present when we use His gifts to us to serve others. It is experienced when we join and support God's family of believers. It is manifested within us when we accept God as the ground of our being and serve Him with joy and thanksgiving. The Kingdom of God is real; it is here and now; it is within us. We can have it anytime we seek it.

2

THE GREATEST COMMANDMENT

"Love the Lord your God with all your heart, and with all your soul, and with all your mind. This is the greatest and the most important commandment." Mt 22:37b-38. (GNB)

". . . Love your enemies, do good to those who hate you, bless those who curse you, and pray for those who mistreat you." Lk: 6:27b-28. (NIV)

God's redemptive plan for our lives is based wholly on love. Why love? Because it is the only religious sentiment that is completely expressed in positive concern for the well-being of others. God wants us to use the criterion of love in determining the goodness of all that we think, feel, and do. When we love God with all our being, it dominates our emotions and directs our thoughts and actions. It becomes the central dynamic of our lives. Love is what we are; love is what we do.

The word love is most commonly used as a verb, e.g., "We love God." It is also widely used as a noun as when we speak of our love for God. Viewing love as a kind of behavior enables us to look at it in terms of its motives and consequences. It is a psychological truism that all human behavior is motivated. This means that everything we do is done to satisfy a need we have. With this thought in mind, let's look at the question of why we love God.

One possible reason is because we are commanded to love Him. But loving God out of a sense of compulsion or fear is contrary to the spirit of love and the nature of God. Love of God is loving only when it is freely given without any sense of coercion or ulterior motive. Love is given for the sake of the loved one and not the lover. Loving God is behaving in ways which are consistent with his expectations of us. Our lives become a testimonial of our love. It is through our love for God that we identify with Him and accept His will as our own. It means, simply, that we want to please him. Our love for God is an empty gesture, however, unless we can commit ourselves to keep his commandments and faithfully observe the guidelines he has established for us. It is through our love of

God that we identify with Him and accept His will as our own.

Dr. Erich Fromm (*The Art of Loving* 1956) has written that love of God is the only passion that can satisfy our need to be in union with someone outside ourselves who is greater than we are. Love is the only answer to the question of how we can, at the same time, be united with God and also maintain a sense of integrity and individuality. Love of God doesn't result in a lessening of the self but an enlargement; it doesn't mean a giving but a receiving. If we don't love God, we turn inward, incurring all kinds of psychic wounds which never heal until we return to God and receive his forgiveness.

The most immediate consequence of loving God and all people here on earth is our enlightenment about the meaning of love. Loving God provides us a sense of security, a serenity, a peace of mind which directs our attention and concern to the more ennobling callings of life. Love lifts us above the sinfulness of our secular lives and causes a fuller unfolding of our potentials. Loving God enriches our human experience and shows how to become all that God intended us to be.

Trust and commitment are critical pre-conditions of our love of God. Trust, which is closely related to faith, is our belief that God is who He claims to be and that He is both able and willing to forgive us of our sins and reconcile us to Him. Trust is an act of faith; it opens the door and invites us to commit our well-being to God. Our commitment to love Him means that we are giving nothing less than our selves—our lives, our destiny—to him.

In our romantic relationships—the domain of eros—we typically refrain from declaring our love for another until the other person has shown some sign of loving us in return. Unlike our earthly love relations, God's love is prevenient. God is love and everywhere God is there is love. In this sense we could paraphrase the Genesis story (Chapter 1, verse 1) to read, "In the beginning love . . ." God's love is unconditional. He doesn't wait for us to love; He loves in anticipation. Although He claims us as His own, He wants to belong to us—to be accepted, to experience relationships with us. God understands, even if we don't, that loving more means being loved more. What goes around comes around.

Through His love for us, God shows His concern for our well-being; He shares His strength and understanding with us to enhance our lives and, in turn, the lives of others. All this He does without denying our freedom to reject His love. Truly, His love is unconditional.

3

THE SECOND GREATEST COMMANDMENT

"'*Love the Lord your God with all your heart, and with all your soul, and with all your mind.' This is the greatest and the most important commandment. The second most important commandment is like it: 'Love your neighbor as you love yourself.' The whole law of Moses and the teachings of the prophets depend on these two commandments.*" *Matt 22:37b-39. (GNB)*

"*. . . . Love your enemies, do good to those who hate you, bless those who curse you, and pray for those who mistreat you.*" *Luke 6:27b-28. (GNB)*

Obeying God's greatest commandment seems both rational and logical even to reluctant Christians. Why? Because God's love is always returned. This idea of exchange satisfies even the skeptic's sense of fairness. In complying

9

with the second greatest commandment, however, we are commanded to love our neighbor without any assurance that our neighbor will love us in return.

Fortunately for us, God doesn't think the way we do about such things as fairness and systems of exchange. His nature is love; He cannot not love. What He wants us to do is to love the way He loves, for only by loving as He loves can we begin to be like Him. When love is given with the expectation of receiving love in return it becomes manipulative and self-serving. What we do receive from loving our neighbor is enlightenment about who our neighbor is. And if we love the way God loves we can help others to experience the power of redeeming love.

However, I suspect that our attitude is much like the lawyer who asked Jesus who his neighbor was. We might also want to know what it means to love our neighbor. Our neighbor is any other member of God's family here on earth. There are no boundaries which separate neighbors from non-neighbors. There are no social or economic distinctions. Our neighbor is any person, anywhere, who needs our love, help, assistance, prayers, whatever. It is never enough to simply say, "I love you?"

We tend to think of love as a relationship between two individuals: the loved and the lover. Our love for our marriage partner is an example. Ideally, these love relationships are reciprocal, meaning that each person both gives and receives love. However, as Dr. Erich Fromm (*The Art of Loving*, 1956) points out, if we love only one other person and are indifferent to the needs of our neighbor, our love is not love in the Biblical sense but only a symbiotic attachment to our loved person.

Mature, Christian love for our neighbors and our enemies is an attitude of active concern for their well-being. It is more than mere passive desires and wishes for their well-being. To be actively concerned we must be doers.

God's commandment to love our neighbor is positive. It is a commandment to love, not a commandment to refrain from hating. It is a relatively easy matter not to hate but the absence of hate in our hearts does not mean the presence of love. To intentionally love our neighbors—some we don't like, many we don't know—requires both a commitment of our will and a pure heart.

It is not enough to merely refrain from hating when there is a need to love. In many human situations we can avoid wrongdoing by doing nothing. In other situations to do nothing is to do wrong. Failing to understand this distinction was the error of the Pharisees. They twisted God's commandment to "Love your neighbor" and interpreted it to mean that they had to love only their neighbors. Since enemies were not mentioned in the commandment, the Pharisees maintained that they had permission, even an injunction, to hate their enemies. They eased the burden of compliance further by defining a neighbor in a very narrow sense. It was this perversion of His commandment that Jesus condemned in His sermon on the mountain.

There is an aspect of Jesus' commandment that causes a lot of undue concern for many Christians. It's the part about "loving yourself." It is widely believed that while loving God and our neighbors is a virtue, loving ourselves is a vice. Self-love, according to this belief, not only reveals a shameful lack of humility but also prevents us from loving others. To some people, we behave as Christians, in part, by belittling or disparaging the self. This is unfortunate since Jesus seems to be saying that without love for the self, we cannot love others. We cannot give to others something that we don't have. Selfish, self-centered people, admittedly, cannot love others, but they have no love for themselves either. Selfishness and self-love, far from being identical, are actually contradictory. When we are able to love as God does, we love both the self and others.

4

BORN AGAIN

"No one can see the Kingdom of God unless he is born again." Jn 3b.(GNB)

The before and after schema is widely used to depict changes in a person, object, or circumstance as a result of some prescribed intervention. Anti-wrinkle creams, diets, and interior decorators use this scheme to show us the situation before and after use of their product or service. Their before-and-after arguments can be very persuasive. The same schema can be used to show the spiritual condition of a person before and after being born again. Jesus is the intervention.

During my years as psychology professor at the Air Force Academy I observed the annual arrival of new cadets to begin their freshman year. First, they were stripped of their civilian dress and demeanor (They were taught to say, "Sir.") Within a few short hours they were transformed from their civilian status to their new military status. Now, they all wore the same uniform, they all had the same haircut, they looked alike, and were subject to the same rules of behavior. There was a transformation; they were made over.

A similar transformation occurred when Lenora and I married. Our professed love and marital oath helped us to make the change from single to married status. We were transformed. Yes, we had problems but with God's help we made it work for fifty-nine glorious years.

To help us better understand the process of being born again ("being born above") let's imagine a two-room house with a single door connecting the first and second rooms. From the first room we can see the sign over the door to the second room which reads simply "Eternal Life." Before we became Christians, beginning with our physical birth, we lived in the first room. We lived what C. S. Lewis called ordinary lives—natural lives, characterized by self-centered thinking and doing. It was a life concerned with satisfying our individual desires and interests. We knew the difference between right and wrong, and possibly felt that we could continue to live our self-centered lives and still have a passing grade as a good person, The sign over the door to Room 2 was not consciously considered; it was a room of unknowns and mysteries. Yet, something in the other room seemed to have a claim on our natural self. We were confused. We were both attracted to and repelled by the mystery of the other room. Were we perhaps tiring of and moving away from the emptiness of Room One or were we strangely moving toward the promise of Room 2, being pulled by some mysterious force that wouldn't let us go? Whatever, it was interfering with our efforts to live good, natural lives—the kind that Nicodemus (Jn 3) fancied himself as living.

Sunday School children sing a song that helps us to see the choice we face. The message of the song is that both bullfrogs and butterflies necessarily undergo a dramatic transformation. The bullfrog starts out as a tadpole; the butterfly starts out as a caterpillar. In order to become what God wants them to be there must be a "new birth." Without it the tadpole never becomes a frog and the caterpillar never becomes a butterfly.

In order to become what God wants us to be we must turn our backs to the natural life of Room One and claim the spiritual life of Room 2. What we thought was a mystery is really simple. Jesus is on the other side of the door, constantly reaching out to us, loving us in spite of our sins. The Holy Spirit is also present, working on us, inviting us to walk through the door. What is involved? First, we must desire to enter the other room. We cannot live in both rooms, we must choose. But passage into the Room of Eternal Life is not something we can do on our own. What we can and must do is recognize our many sins, confess them to God, and pray for His forgiveness. A variety of terms is used to describe what happens next. Jesus said we must be born again—a spiritual birth, from above. With this new birth we profess our belief in Jesus as our Savior and accept the Holy Spirit into our lives. There are traditions that refer to this process as being saved or being converted. All these terms refer to each other. The process is symbolized by our being baptized which, in turn, is traditionally accompanied by our affiliation with a congregation of Jesus' church here on earth.

As believers we receive God's forgiveness when we repent of our sins and profess our faith in Jesus Christ for salvation.

In response God is prepared and ready to forgive all our sins: big, small, past, present, and future. We will continue to sin after we are saved; we will never be free from sin until we die. The thought of scripture is not that we will never sin again but that we are not going to make a practice of it. Yes, we will sin again but as often as we confess our sins God is faithful to forgive them. We preserve and strengthen our spiritual nature by prayer, Bible study, and uniting with a body of believers (church) who worship God in spirit and in truth.

5

ADULTERY

"Do not commit adultery." Exodus 20:14. (GNB)

"You have heard that it was said, 'Do not commit adultery.' But now I tell you: anyone who looks at a woman and wants to possess her is guilty of committing adultery with her in his heart." Mt 5:27-28. (GNB)

After creating male and female humans in his own image, God blessed them and commanded them to "Be fruitful and multiply." (Genesis 1:26-28). God's gift of sexual love within marriage provided a way for us to cooperate with Him in the multiplication process, in terms of passion, fidelity, and integrity. But, after observing humans' proclivity toward sexual excesses, God realized that if His human family was to survive and flourish some restrictions would have to be forced upon human sexual behavior. First, God established the family and ordained that sexual intercourse was prohibited outside the bonds of marriage. Everywhere, whatever its form, the institution of the family has found it necessary to establish rules regarding the sexual behavior of its members. So basic, so apparent is this need that it is supported by custom and law. God put the force of His authority behind what people in families everywhere would know what is expected of them. We must realize that, of all life's pleasures, sex can have by far the most serious consequence, i.e., pregnancy—a consequence which only the family is prepared to accept and nurture.

Second, God prohibited adultery and the secret desire for sexual partners other than one's spouse (Exodus 20:14 and 17). Can anyone argue against God's prohibition against adultery? No. His commandment is simple and clear; it is practical, wise, and loving. Our conscience tells us that adultery is wrong. Any reasonable person, villain or victim, can testify to the inevitable, abusive consequences of adultery upon a marriage and family stability, some immediate, some delayed. Had this taboo, along with the taboo against premarital sex, not have been accepted family members, especially young females, could not be protected against sexual predators. Even with the taboo, rape and sexual battery occur with alarming frequency. Sexual violation of another person is less a sexual act than an acting out of power and control. Satisfying one's sexual needs at the expense of another person, even in marriage, is a sin.

When practiced outside of marriage, sex can, and often does, lead to all sorts of degradations and perversities. A permissive society can argue that one's private behavior is one's own personal business. But history proves them wrong: private behavior has public consequences. Strictly speaking, adultery is never private. Unlike other sins, adultery requires the cooperation of another person. Two active participants, yes, but what about their spouses? Spouses who are betrayed, lied to, and victimized? Spouses who are being robbed of commitment and intimacy? And children? A parent who cannot tell a child where they were last night is alienated from them

During my twenty-five years of practice as a psychotherapist I heard every imaginable recitation about people's efforts to either rationalize or deal with the guilt and shame of their adultery. Adultery is both a moral and a mental health issue; it breaks both God's law and the human heart. Theologically speaking, adultery is a violation of God's law; violators are punished for their sin. Psychologically speaking, adultery violates the integrity of the human personality; violators are punished by their guilt.

Our problem with sex is not that we think too highly of it, but that we don't think of it highly enough. Compared to the myths and lies of our contemporary culture about sex, only marital fidelity keeps us focused on God's plan for sex in our lives.

6

AMBITION

"Don't do anything from selfish ambition or from a cheap desire to boast, but be humble toward one another, always considering others better than yourself. And look out for one another's interest, not your own." Phil 2:3-4. (GNB)

The military triumphs of Julius Caesar, Emperor of Rome, were being celebrated at the annual feat of Lupercali. Not everyone was celebrating, however. Some dissatisfied noblemen were discussing with concern Caesar's growing power and incurable ambition. In another of Shakespeare's plays, *Henry VIII*, the prologue introduces the play as being sad in its reality of ambition, self-aggrandizement, and political maneuvering. Ambition, it seems, was the stuff of Shakespeare's dramas but it enjoyed a less favorable reputation off stage.

Outside the theater ambition had little to recommend it.

In some circles this unsavory perception of ambition persists. To describe someone as ambitious conjures up a litany of uncomplimentary, negative images. Beware of ambition, it is argued, for it is like the proverbial camel's nose. Once the camel gets its nose into your tent you have to deal with the whole camel. In the case of ambition it's the consequences that are analogous to the rest of the camel: selfishness, win-at-all-costs attitudes, deception, etc.

All behavior is motivated behavior—it does not occur in a vacuum—and is directed toward satisfying individual needs. Whether ambition is good or bad is always determined by the consequences it produces. Ambition is neutral and can be either good or bad depending upon the goals of the actor and the consequences of the behavior for other persons.

When ambition is perceived as self-serving it is judged negatively, e.g.' power seeking, control, and self-aggrandizement. The purest form of ambition is political because its focus is to rule or control other people. These seekers endeavor to satisfy their own needs without consideration of their consequences of their behavior on others. In fact, they may satisfy their own needs at the expense of others. When ambition is perceived as having desirable social consequences it is judged to be positive and desirable. The apostle Paul wrote "It is my ambition to preach the good news . . . ." (Rom 15:20). Andrew Carnegie (early leader of US Steel) declared his desire (ambition) to make as much money as he could so he could endow hospitals and libraries. Paul and Carnegie were motivated to help others and the benefits of their efforts are appreciated today.

The accepted definition of ambition is, fortunately, changing—if not actually changing it is being perceived as softer and less negative than in the past. If this process of change continues there is hope that it will soon become more respectable. Can you imagine a person with no ambition at all? Why bother to get out of bed in the morning? Why bother to satisfy physical needs, even less so to satisfy higher order needs? The Bible condemns both too much ambition and too little ambition. Too much involves a lot of attitudes and behavior that are abhorrent to God as does too little, although for different reasons. Too much is synonymous with greed, selfishness, and a lack of consideration of others. Too little ambition results in laziness, lost opportunities, free-loading behavior and an irresponsible attitude that society owes everyone a living. Is there a middle ground that would negate the unchristian outcomes of both extremes? Is ambition an all or nothing idea? Is it like the Biblical story of separating the sheep from the goats? I prefer to answer this question by recognizing that ambition, like money, is neither good nor bad: it is inherently neutral. What makes it good or bad is the focus or purpose to which ambitious behavior is directed, how it is used.

Michael Kinsley's essay in *Time* (14Jan07) addresses the question of "Why They (presidential candidates) Run?" His answer is "Ladies and Gentlemen, they are running because they are ambitious . . . . This doesn't make them bad, it makes them human." Kinsley continues by observing that ambition can never be naked (least of all in the political arena), it must be clothed in deceit.

Kinsleys's conclusion reminds us of the adage "Oh what tangled webs we weave when first we choose to deceive." Deceiving is lying and lying violates God's Commandment. Deception is a consequence of ambition gone awry.

7

ANGER

"If you become angry, do not let your anger lead you into sin, and do not stay angry all day. Don't give the devil a chance." Eph 4:26-27. (GNB)

On May 3, 1980, Candance Lightener's thirteen-year old daughter, Cari, was killed by an drunken hit-and-run driver on a suburban street in California. Put yourself in the mother's circumstances. Might she have felt anger? Yes. Might she have wanted revenge? Probably. What did she do? "I promised on the day of Cari's death that I would make her death count for something in the future."

Mrs. Lightener founded MADD (Mothers Against Drunk Driving) with the twin objectives of eliminating drunk driving and preventing under-age drinking. Today, there are chapters of MADD around the world. Mrs. Lightener's response to her daughter's death provided two important lessons for us in learning to deal with our anger. First, anger is an emotional response to an offending event or circumstance. It energizes us to change the anger-provoking situation. Second, she taught us that anger doesn't have to end in violence. It can be used for good or bad, depending upon how we respond. Understandably, anger is a much misunderstood emotion.

Everybody gets angry occasionally. I do and I suppose that you do, too. It is human nature. In one way or another we all have problems with anger. Sometimes it is expressed as a quiet seething resentment or indignation at some large or small offense, real or imagined. This is common since we have been taught to fear anger. When we realize we are angry we may also feel frightened and try to laugh it off or pretend it doesn't matter. At other times we may attempt to justify our anger rather than accept responsibility for it. At other times anger explodes into vindictive, self-serving behavior directed toward offending persons or circumstances. In either case, realizing and accepting our anger is necessary for constructive resolution.

The Bible teaches that anger can be but is not, *ipso facto,* a sin of mental attitude. It stops short of condemning all anger. Paul preached, "Be ye angry, and sin not." (Eph 4:26). Anger is sinful when it is selfishly motivated, when it seeks to harm or demean

others through either causing or wishing
them evil. The term "righteous indignation"
is used to describe anger directed against
an unholy situation, e.g., injustice, child
abuse, and hunger. It is unselfish and directed
toward benefitting others who, often, cannot
change the situation themselves. We can fight
injustice without being angry; we need not
fear anger when it is righteous. Moses was
angered when he came down from Mt. Sinai and
saw the people dancing and singing in honor
of an idol. (Ex 32:19).

Did Moses sin? Jesus angrily drove the
money changers from the temple. (Mt 21:12-13).
Did Jesus sin? Both Moses and Jesus expressed
anger without sinning. Their anger had the
quality of being righteous, it was provoked
by the need to change an unholy situation.
Failing to act as they did would have produced
a sinful effect. Righteous indignation may be
and often is a result of holiness itself.

What are we to do with our unrighteous
anger? Our instinctive manner of expressing
anger is to respond aggressively—it is a
natural, adaptive response to perceived
threats against our well-being. A certain
amount of anger is necessary for survival.
But we can't aggressively lash out at everyone
who angers us. What can we do?

Behaviorally, we can choose to express our
anger, suppress our anger, or calm ourselves

inside until the anger feelings subside. The calming technique seldom works. We may think we have our anger under control without realizing that our eyes and facial expressions reveal the inside emotion of anger. Trying to deny our anger when we are perceived by others as being angry raises real questions of honesty and trust. Attempting to suppress our anger—not allowing outward expression—poses the danger of turning it inside where it can result in possible depression and also lead to resentment and avoidance of the person or situation causing the anger. Sharing our angry feelings in an assertive, non-aggressive manner is, psychologically, the healthiest choice we can make.

As a psychotherapist I have helped patients admit to and accept ownership of their angry feelings using this scenario: "I do have anger feelings toward you and I don't like it. I don't want to feel angry toward you. I won't try to deny my feelings because my face and tone of voice would give me away. We both know that it's hard to trust someone we perceive as being angry when they are denying their anger. Could we sit down and talk about it?" This approach produces positive results because it respects both ourself and the other.

It's OK to get angry; it is not OK to sin. Anger is truly a much misunderstood emotion.

8

ANXIETY

"Therefore do not be anxious, saying 'What shall we eat?' or 'What shall we drink?' or 'What shall we wear?' . . . . But seek first His Kingdom and His righteousness, and all these things shall be yours as well." Mt. 6:31 and 33. (RSV)

"So do not be anxious about anything, but in everything, by prayer and petition, present your requests to God and the peace of God which transcends all understanding will guard your hearts and minds in Christ." Phil 4:6-7. (RSV)

Many versions of the Bible use the word worry for the word anxious in the above citations. I chose the Revised Standard Version citations because I want to emphasize an important difference between worry and anxiety. Although I will focus on anxiety alone, it is emphasized that anxiety seldom happens in isolation. There is a lot of interdependence between anxiety and other problem emotions such as worry, fear, hostility, anger, and resentment. They love to keep company

Anxiety can be thought of as a psychic pain that serves a protective function. In the same sense that physical pain tells us something is wrong, anxiety signals that all is not well emotionally. Anxiety results from real or imagined threats to our well-being but, unlike physical pain, and other problem emotions, anxiety is more vague and diffused. In chapter 65, *Worry,* I wrote that our conscious fears of adverse happenings cause us to worry about their consequences. The assumption is that we are aware of our worrying and the causes of it. We allow—often even cause—ourselves worry. Because the source of our anxiety is unclear and often beyond our level of consciousness it is more difficult to understand and attack than is worry. The negative effects are evident, however, since anxiety causes us to feel vulnerable and unprotected without knowing why and is typically accompanied by feelings of insecurity, helplessness, and isolation. When we experience anxiety, our metabolism speeds up, our muscles tighten, and our adrenal glands produce extra adrenaline, preparing our bodies for fight or flight. Prolonged anxiety, beyond a very minimal level, keeps our bodies mobilized for emergency responses, possibly causing both psychological and physical problems. Finally, and most importantly, especially to God, anxiety robs us of much of the joy of living.

Psychotherapists treat anxiety with counselling and, when appropriate, medications. Jesus treats anxiety with faith and prayer. These two approaches are both valid and effective and in my practice of psychotherapy I considered them complementary. Just as faith is prerequisite to prayer; faith, or believing in the efficacy of therapy, is necessary for both therapist and patient if psychological healing is to occur.

When we consider the incidence of anxiety disorders in our modern society we are tempted to believe that it is endemic to the present age. Biblical history supports a contrary conclusion. From the beginning, from Genesis to Revelation, the Bible is replete with examples of anxiety and other problem emotions. the people of the Bible faced many of the same anxieties and stresses we do today. Problems of welfare, health, safety, and family relations were just as real then as now, and the effects of anxiety were just as profound. During the life of Jesus the uncertainties and frustrations of living under Roman domination only exacerbated the peoples' everyday anxieties.

Jesus observed that anxiety disorders were capable of controlling our thought processes and distorting our perceptions of life. Yet, this is contrary to what He wants for us. He wants to give us His joy and His peace, He never intended for us to live a life of anxiety and worry. He clearly told us not to be anxious about life and its necessities. He wants us to come to Him in faith and prayer, trusting Him to provide these things for us. He clearly saw how it could disrupt our lives, cloud our decision making, and sap us of our spiritual strength. Jesus wants us to trust Him; He wants to replace our anxiety and worry with His peace and joy.

9

APPEARANCE

". . . the Lord doesn't make decisions the way you do. People judge by outward appearance, the Lord looks at a person's thoughts and intentions."
(1 Sam 16:7b)

It was Sunday and I was in church again, sitting in my accustomed pew next to the center aisle. I was there every Sunday.

Congregants were still entering the sanctuary as the prelude was being played. I looked over the worship bulletin and marked the hymnal pages and the Bible citations for both the Old Testament Lesson and the Gospel Lesson. Then the organist stopped playing and the liturgist welcomed everyone and made a few announcements not included in the bulletin. Things moved quickly and soon it was time for the sermon. I was pleased—the Falcons football game telecast was scheduled to begin at two o'clock. Lunch and the drive home could push me.

After providing some background about the story of Jesus' encounter with the Samaritan woman at the well (John 4) the pastor invited our attention to verses 23 and 24. I followed along, reading from my Bible. I knew those verses well, about worshiping God in spirit and truth, but today I stopped at the words "true worshippers" in verse 23. Strange. I had always moved quickly to verse 24, believing that was the meat of Jesus' teaching. Indeed, the pastor repeated verse 24, indicating that it would be the focus of his sermon. Maybe I was feeling a tinge of guilt for being concerned about the football game, but the words "true worshipper" held my attention. "What is a true worshipper?" I pondered. "Aren't all worshippers true?" Apparently not, else Jesus would not have used the adjective true to describe worshippers. Was I a true worshiper? Do I really worship God during the hour we call worship? Why was the pastor not addressing this point?

Being a true worshiper (verse 23) is a precondition to worshiping God in spirit and truth (verse 24). We naturally think that people who come to church come to truly worship God in spirit and truth. But I know from my own experience that there is a lot that happens during worship that is not true worship. Jesus was aware of this circumstance when He quoted Isaiah in warning us that "These people honor Me with their lips, but their hearts are far from Me (Mark 7:6)." Jesus was telling us that much of what we call worship is not acceptable to Him. We feign worship without focusing solely on God and this calls our motives into question. Do we want to please others or God? One of the great temptations we face in worship is to act piously—create a favorable appearance—in order to gain the approval of others. We erroneously believe that by creating a good appearance we can control what others think of us. We can become so good at faking our worship experiences that we mistakenly believe we can fool even Jesus. But Jesus is not fooled nor is He impressed.

It has been said that in prayer we are concerned with our needs, in thanksgiving we are occupied with our blessings, but in true worship we are focused on God. We owe worship to God; it is His due. If we don't truly worship God in spirit and truth we are robbing Him of His due. It is not enough that we obey Him, that we pray to Him, that we give Him thanks, that we seek to serve Him and do His will. We must truly worship God.

How simple our lives would if we were just honest with ourselves and with God. Why are we so afraid to be honest with God? Why do we try so hard to create an appearance that we think would cause others to think favorably of us? We might fool others for a while but faking piety does not fool God. God is simply not impressed with such behavior. God knows what is in our hearts.

The essence of worship of God is genuineness. It can be likened to standing spiritually naked before God, praying for His spirit to "plug" into our spirit and open the door for true worship. We must be willing to let the Spirit lead us in our worship. Our worship of God must be simple and true. It must come from the heart, a spiritual worship. We must please God, not ourselves, not others.

10

ARROGANCE

"No one is respected unless he is humble; arrogant people are on the way to ruin." Prov 18:12. (GNB)

A package in the morning mail contained a copy of *The King James Bible*. The sender was not identified. A brief hand-written note attached to the Bible read, "I saw your article in the newspaper. You made a reference to *The Message*. That is not a real Bible. I will pray for you." I was confused. I wanted to defend my reference. I felt anger. The gall of this person to judge me. Did the sender know something that I didn't? Was the sender arrogant? Was I?

On the January 3, 2010, Fox Sunday News Program Britt Hume, a Fox Senior News Analyst, advised scandal-plagued Tiger Woods to "turn to Christianity (from Buddhism) to achieve total recovery." Accusations of Hume's arrogance were immediate. Was Brit Hume arrogant? Did he owe Mr. Woods an apology?

Arrogance is an ugly word. We retreat from it and try to avoid its imagery. It is full of badness and empty of goodness. Consider the company it keeps: its synonyms include self-righteousness, authoritarianism, manipulation, self-centeredness, coercion, obstinacy, etc. It is ugly because it leaves no room for humility and respect for others. An arrogant person asserts his views, values, and knowledge as superior to those of others and they must be respected, and defended when challenged. Arrogance is ugly when we see it in others; it is painful when we fall victim to it.

Arrogance is more than having a high opinion of one's talents and abilities. It stands apart from the self-confident person who does indeed have considerable knowledge and abilities and is aware of the fact. There is nothing more admirable than the self-confident person who can share his beliefs while respecting the beliefs of others. Self-confident persons never insist that you are wrong and that they are right. However, self-confidence can easily be confused with arrogance, especially when articulated in logical seemingly well thought-out terms. Arrogance goes beyond healthy self-confidence. What is the boundary? Arrogance goes beyond healthy self-confidence when it becomes destructive of human relationships. An arrogant person fails to respect this boundary.

My late wife and I always enjoyed entertaining our friends and neighbors with sit-down dinners. Characteristically, when our guests were seated and thanks given to God for the food and the occasion, she would again welcome them with the invitation to eat and drink with joy and thanksgiving. Then, she would good naturedly (and wisely) suggest that discussion of politics and religion was off limits at dinner.

Feelings about politics and religion are fused with value and weighted with emotion. These feelings are also highly individualistic; we identify with them and are quick to defend them when challenged or slighted, especially in the area of religious beliefs and practices. Our most well-intentioned and innocent remarks can be easily interpreted by others in terms of their personal beliefs and past experiences. This can open the door to exchanges of spiritual arrogance. We deceive ourselves when we argue that we are not like that. It is but another—not lesser—form of arrogance to believe otherwise. Arrogance drives people apart when we try to disguise our arrogance as a virtue. Consider, for example, the attitude of the Pharisee who thanked God that he was not like other men . . . . (Lk

18:11). Or, consider the Pharisees as a group, who were blinded by their arrogance as to who Jesus was (Mt 9:34). Without denying Jesus' healing powers they pointed to a demonic source. All the time, they believed they were upholding the Law.

Arrogance and its close cousin, pride, can cause us untold misery, leaving us feeling lonely, both socially and spiritually. Jesus preached a gospel of humility and love. He taught that the "proud will be humbled, but the humble will be honored." (Lk 14:17) Spiritual arrogance substitutes a self-centered self-righteousness for God's gospel of truth.

11

CHASTITY

"God wants you to be holy and completely free from sexual immorality." 1 Thes 4:3. (GNB)

Imagine what it would be like living in a society where chastity was an unknown virtue. Our first thought would be that such a society could not long exist. The erosion of the foundations of society—family, values, law, traditions, etc.,—would doom any society that turns its back on this virtue. God wisely realized the inevitable injurious consequences and commanded us to refrain from such behavior. As Christians, we accept God's commandments on faith. Still, we might ponder the reason for God's commandments against sexual immorality. Rules should have reasons and God's reasons for his rules governing human sexual conduct center upon what is good for us. God is absolute in His judgments and expects submission from us. Because God's rules are good for us, we understand His reasons and accept them on faith.

The question of definition is preeminent in any discussion of chastity. Asking the question elicits answers like "It's a girl's name" or "I think it's a belt." A more intentioned but flawed answer might be that chastity is the absence of sex. But that is abstinence; it focuses on what we cannot do and cannot have. It also negates further discussion of the need to define chastity. Although the two terms are closely related and are often used interchangeably, chastity goes beyond abstinence—way beyond. Chastity can be equated to sexual purity in the sense that it is a virtue. As a virtue, it defines the content and boundaries of the life style which Jesus calls us to observe—single or married, male or female, young or old. Chastity does not forbid sex; it simply proscribes it outside the married relationship. However, chastity within marriage can be violated by unloving impure thoughts, desires, and words. Mark 7:21-23 is a virtual catalogue of unholy intentions that come from within the heart and defile the purity of love.

While we all face the problem of how to live a chaste life in an unchaste world, the problem is most pressing on unmarried persons, particularly teenagers. During my thirty years of practice as a psychotherapist

I listened to their stories. I hurt with them. We searched for solutions together.

"It seemed so natural."

"We were in love."

"Every body else was doing it."

"He said that if I loved him I would do it."

"If I didn't do it I wouldn't have any friends."

The majority of the stories I heard were told by females, and that is another side of the tragic consequences of premarital sex resulting from emotion rather than reason. The possible consequences run the gambit from pregnancy and sexually transmitted diseases to loss of self-esteem and being thought of as sluttish. It is tragic when persons seeking love see chastity as a barrier. It is tragic when persons seeking love settle for sex. Likewise, it is tragic when males, who would like to be viewed as protectors, deceptively manipulate the wholesomeness of a social relationship for their own self-interest. Finally, it is tragic when the female partner—who is most often the most vulnerable—is left to suffer the possible negative consequences of a relationship gone awry.

The summary of the above argument is that unchaste persons are not really free to love. Until partners in a relationship see each other as persons, selfless love can never flourish. Intentions can be declared and promises made, but in the absence of selfless love—chaste and pure—the relationship remains utilitarian, being pursued for individual, selfish interests.

Chastity can be both desirable and attractive—a thought that is showing some evidence of revival. Vows of chastity, chastity rings, and abstinence worship and discussion groups are today being observed with increasing frequency, particularly on college campuses. These activities and programs portend changing attitudes about chastity as the spiritual, psychological, and physical benefits are recognized. Chastity is a good advertisement for the integrity and purity of one's self. It is a state of wholesomeness and well-being. Chaste persons can proudly say, "I am valuable and worth waiting for. I can stand before the mirror and like what I see."

12

CHRISTIAN IDENTITY

"If you have love for one another, everybody will know you are my disciples." Jn 13:35. *(GNB)*

Who am I?

Everyone has wrestled with this question at one time or another. Although usually thought of as an adolescence concern, it is pervasive, affecting young and old. Since there are no final answers it cannot be laid aside at any age. We are always growing, changing, evolving.

My first and most significant encounter with this question was when I underwent a period of psychoanalysis in preparation for my licensure to practice marriage and family therapy. That was when I really got acquainted with myself. As I discovered who I was as a person, I gained insight into how I thought, felt, and behaved in various social and work situations. Like a series of concentric circles with the self at the center, the discovery process spilled over and provided insights into my role as a husband, as a father, and as a therapist. These early steps in my journey toward self-awareness were both tortuous and exhilarating. Today, I am still shifting the chaff from the grain, still looking for new answers to the question of "Who am I?"

But let us back up a bit. Somewhere along the path of my journey I became aware that something was missing. The sense of wholeness I expected to achieve seemed incomplete. I felt comfortable with my answers to the questions of, "Who am I?" and "Where am I going?", but I had no answers to the ultimate question, "Why?".

What is the purpose and meaning of my life? What significant things can I do with my life? What is my relationship with God? What does my relationship with God mean in terms of how I live my life? What does it mean to be a part of His creation? These were questions to which I did not have answers. They involved values: questions of right and wrong, questions of good and bad, questions about what should be rather than what is. Neither the science that I had studied nor my own past experience could help me. Only my religion was prepared to provide me the answers I knew I needed.

These questions all pointed me to the spiritual dimensions of my life, indicating my need to have a Christian identity. Simply claiming to be a Christian, I knew, was not enough—there had to be a supportive Christian lifestyle. In fact, a Christian identity becomes real only when it proceeds from a lifestyle of Christ-like values, commitment, and behavior.

Three fundamental facts must be woven into the fabric of our Christian identity. First, there is God's act of creation which is closely embraced by the second fact: His plan or purpose for his children. Why did He create us? Why did He give us a model (Jesus), and rules (The Bible) to live our lives by? What does He expect of us? It is at this point where our response—the third fact—meets God's plan. It is here that our Christian identity is born, hopefully resulting in a life of both Christian *being* and *doing*. It is a life that accepts God as the highest value in our existence, requiring us to judge our secular, natural life by God's standard of a spiritual, Christian life. This comparison inevitably leads us to repentance and a realignment of our values and goals with those of God. Having a Christian identity necessarily requires us to subordinate our will to God's will. We must accept God's blueprint for our lives. Once we have a distinct Christian identity, all of our actions are or should be intendedly consistent with it.

A coherent sense of self is a prerequisite to a Christian identity. I am not suggesting that we must first create a physical, natural self. No, this we already have. Rather, it is necessary for us to be aware of who and what we are before we can recognize the need for change. We must know what we are before we can contemplate what we could and should be. People who have an awareness of the self with its weaknesses, faults, tendencies, etc., and a sense of knowing what makes something right and something else wrong, and of being able to choose the right over the wrong, meet the preconditions of a Christian identity more adequately than people who lack this awareness. Having a sense of the self is a necessary but insufficient condition for consciously acquiring a Christian identity.

A Christian identity has both internal dimensions, such as a Christian conscience, and external dimensions, such as a Christian disposition. All people have a conscience, but not all people have a Christian conscience they can trust in choosing to do right and avoiding wrong. A Christian conscience is constantly being cleansed and renewed by confession, repentance, and restitution. The external counterpart to a Christian conscience is a Christian disposition which reflects our temperament or tendency to live by the commandment of love. A person with a disposition to be joyous, unselfish, forgiving, and filled with hope and courage is a good advertisement for God.

13

CHRISTIAN PERFECTION

"You must be perfect—just as your Father in heaven is perfect." Mt 5:48. (GNB)

Perfection: The quality or state of being perfect.

Perfect: Being entirely without fault or flaw.

Faultless and flawless are words that don't come easily to our mind. Indeed, words like these are difficult to vocalize because the occasions for using them, in secular affairs at least, are rare. In business, government, and academia, we have far too long accepted good enough as good enough. We have tolerated the mundane, promoted the average, and rewarded the mediocre. Whatever good enough is, it is something less than our best. In our religious lives, however, good enough is not good enough. Perfection is not only expected, it is commanded.

Some people are bothered by Christ's words: "You must be perfect . . . .". They seem to think that unless they are perfect Christ will not help them. And since they cannot be perfect, they assume their situation is hopeless. "Why bother?" they reason.

Admittedly, Jesus' command to seek perfection, at first reading, does comes across as His most difficult. Could He be serious when He knows there is none among us who even faintly approaches perfection? Yes, He is serious. Yes, He does expect His commandment to be obeyed. If not, why did He make it? Jesus would not command us to do something when He knew we could not, on our own, possibly obey.

I think Christ was also saying, "I will help you to become perfect. I want the Father to be pleased with you just as He was pleased with Me. You may want something else, but the only help I will give you is to help you become perfect." Christ also knows, even if we do not, that of our own efforts we will never get anywhere near perfection. But with Christ, all things are possible. Although we are not now perfect, we are, with His help, perfectible; in Him there is both the possibility and the reality of Christian perfection.

Christian perfection does not mean being without sin. It does mean freedom from intentional, deliberate sin. It means, at a minimum, that we must be perfect in our intentions to love, to forgive, and to practice righteousness. As we move toward perfection we grow in our understanding of God, letting go our early, childish ideas. Our faith becomes more mature and is able to better withstand the buffeting of temptation and doubt. We also grow in awareness of and sensitivity to the working of the Holy Spirit in our lives. We awaken to new opportunities for Christian service; we discover new desire and energy to do God's will. William Barclay, in his commentary on this teaching, suggests that perfection is functional, i.e., we do not seek Christian perfection for perfection's sake. No, perfection has a purpose or goal; it is not an end but a means to a holy end. We move toward perfection, in the New Testament sense of the word, when we recognize and accept the purpose for which we were created. Barclay interprets this purpose as our need to love the way God loves, to forgive the way God forgives. We are on our way to Christian perfection when we demonstrate the characteristics of righteousness and holiness which prepare us for communion with God. Christian perfection was a cardinal doctrine of early Methodism. It is, in fact, today recognized as a special doctrinal contribution of Methodism to the Church universal. John Wesley, who founded (some say inspired) Methodism, emphasized sanctification as a precondition of perfection. Through sanctification we are set apart for a special use by God. Seeking Christian perfection prepares us for that purpose.

Unfortunately, many people practice their religion like they prepared for their courses in college—always concerned about the passing score. How much effort is required to pass (be accepted by God)? They want to know and are willing to settle for a degree of righteousness that is good enough. They may be willing to settle for a C grade (good enough), but Jesus expects us to work for the A grade—perfection. Seeking perfection is a renunciation of doing just enough to get by.

The word perfection has some unfortunate semantic connotations since it tends to suggest a final, fixed state of being. It is a goal, yes, but it has no determined ending point. If we can live one hour or one day without sin, we become a new person—growing in grace, maturing in love and forgiveness—strengthened for the next hour or day. If we can live one hour or day without sin, why not two hours or two days? Why not all our hours and days?

14

COMPASSION

"If there is any encouragement in Christ, any consolation from love, any sharing of the Spirit, any compassion and sympathy, make my joy complete; be of the same mind, having the same love, being in full accord and of one mind." Phil 2:1-2 (NRSV)

An anonymous, often-quoted definition of compassion is " . . . the bone you throw to the dog when you are as hungry as the dog." This definition is attractive because it evidences a willingness to suffer with another to the degree that you forget about your own needs and spontaneously do what love and empathy demand. This definition would be even more attractive if the bone had been shared. By giving the bone, the giver is trading circumstances with the receiver. An element of enlightened judgment would suggest that by sharing the bone, the lot of the receiver would be improved without totally depriving the giver. Will the receiver of the bone obey the law of compassion? Will the storehouse of goodness be enlarged by the exchange of the bone?

Compassion is a personal awareness of our encounter with another person who is hurting, lacking, or struggling and we have the wherewithal and desire to help. Compassion is not a stand-alone virtue; it reveals the depth and sincerity of our desire to love. Love is a verb. We love others; it is also something we do. If the goal of the Christian life is love, without compassion it misses the goal. Help, likewise, is a verb. We help others; it is also something we do. Compassion is a noun; it motivates us to behave toward others with an understanding of and sympathy for their circumstances. Love without compassion is not agape love. If we help others without compassion, we run the risk of serving our own needs.

Compassion is a profound, pervasive human emotion, prompted by the pain and needs of others (including animals). Compassion strengthens love; it is more rigorous than empathy, and it enlarges the boundaries of altruism. Compassion motivates loving, caring behavior. In ethical terms, compassion is taught as a natural, heartfelt pervading virtue. It is rooted in the hearts of religious persons and defended as a cardinal virtue in all major religious traditions. The individual who denies or refuses to show compassion is characterized as evil. To deny love and compassion is to align ourselves with a cold, uncaring world.

In our Christian heritage Paul begins his second letter to the Corinthians (1:3), by describing God as the "Father of Compassion," and as the "God of all Comfort." Our heritage embodies the very essence of compassion as Jesus teaches us to forsake our own desires and to act compassionately toward others. In His Sermon on the Mount, Jesus promises that the merciful (compassionate) would receive mercy (Mt 5:7). In His parable of the Good Samaritan (Lk 10:29-37) Jesus taught the ideal of compassion. Numerous other instances can be cited of Jesus being moved with compassion; it was evident in all His acts of healing.

Norman Cousins, the author of <u>The Anatomy of an Illness</u> (1959), opined that as individuals we are capable of both great compassion and great indifference. We also have it within our means to nourish compassion and outgrow indifference. Everyone is capable of compassion, yet many of us avoid it because we are not always able to act out our feelings. We avoid watching the evening news because it confronts us with our limitations. Our sense of compassion is easily aroused, but our feelings of being unable to respond directly leave us with a psychic numbness. We are not indifferent; we are hopeless. To avoid the pangs of psychological guilt, we seek to avoid the guilt-producing stories of famine, crime, deprivation, etc., that are reported daily.

Is there a limit to our compassion? Can we open our heart to every condition that begs for compassionate understanding and change. Can we choose not to be open to experience the pain of others? If it is a matter of judgment, on what basis do we make our decisions? What values guide us in deciding? Our ability to practice compassion may at times be overwhelmed by the demands of the situation. When this happens, we must share our feelings with God and pray for His guidance. All things are possible with God.

15

CONFLICT

"What causes fights and quarrels among you? Don't they come from your desires that battle within you? You want something but don't get it. You kill and covet, but you cannot have what you want. You quarrel and fight. You do not have, because you do not ask God." Jam 4:1-2. (NIV)

We traditionally view conflict in churches as disruptive and contrary to the norms of Christian behavior. It is something to be avoided. When it does happen, it should be resolved as quickly and quietly as possible. If people truly loved God and sought to live by His commandments, we reason, there would naturally result an abiding sense of love and cooperation. People who fail to live by these precepts are characterized as hypocrites, trouble makers, prima donnas, etc.

A more contemporary view of conflict in churches is that it is neither good nor bad. It is, rather, a natural condition that occurs because we differ in our ways of thinking, feeling, and behaving. It occurs because we view situations in terms of our individual values, goals, and expectations. It occurs because we care. Conflict is an inevitable characteristic of the closeness and interdependence of people in churches.

Conflict can be usefully defined as a perceived condition that exists between people in which there is both an incompatibility of goals and an opportunity by one person or group to interfere with the goals and accomplishments of others. Conflict is not an objective set of conditions or circumstances existing apart from people. Rather, it is a set of conditions or circumstances that is perceived to exist or that is perceived to be evolving.

Sometimes, conflict is viewed as the opposite of cooperation. In a limited sense this is true, since people in conflict see their goals as being incompatible, and people who are cooperating see their goals as being mutually supportive. However, the absence of conflict does not assure cooperation, just as the absence of cooperation does not mean the presence of conflict.

Can two honest, moral people hold opposing views about a problem faced by their church?

Yes. Is it possible for parishioners to divide into opposing factions over changing situations in their church? Yes.

In one church, parishioners identified themselves as either fundamentalists or liberals in relation to a number of social issues being debated by their church. It had a humorous dimension to it until they started sitting on the right or left side of the aisle according to the political connotation of their respective labels. The problem escalated to the point where the pastor left in frustration.

A small country church was located near a growing residential complex. New residents of the area who started attending the century-old church were accused by the old timers of "taking over our church."

A man and woman whose spouses had died within weeks of each other decided to marry after a brief courtship. Their pastor refused to marry them until an appropriate period of mourning had elapsed. His refusal to marry them was both defended and censured. The two people who wanted to marry were both applauded and criticized; the pastor who refused to marry them was both defended and verbally censured. Other congregations have experienced conflict over whether to build a new sanctuary, whether to permit guitars in their worship, and whether to permit divorced parishioners to serve in leadership roles of the church.

Compromise is often pictured as the easiest and most practical solution to church conflict. It permits contending parties to experience both some winning and some losing. On the other hand, it denies all parties getting what they really want. It invites unrealistic demands and expectations by the parties and also serves to prevent an airing of the real issues in the conflict. Withdrawal (in the manner of Pontius Pilate), controlling, and accommodation are other approaches with both advantages and disadvantages. Collaboration is the appropriate style for resolving conflict and restoring unity in church congregations. It takes time, skill, and patience, but it has the advantage of providing the overall best solutions.

Both prayer and the Bible are ever-ready sources of discernment and strength which are available to would-be conflict mediators and peacemakers. Both give us insight and strength for dealing with conflict. The Bible, it seems, can relate to us in every condition of human life. It helps us to look at conflict more realistically, with understanding, without judgment. Through prayer we can consult with the wisest and most supportive helper we can ever have, and, if we pause long enough for God to speak to us, we are helped to understand the issues in conflict and to deal with them more honestly in a trusting and supportive climate.

16

COVETING

"Do not covet another man's house; do not covet his wife, his slaves, his donkeys, or anything else that he owns." Ex 20:17. (GNB)

The word covet has seemingly disappeared from our moral landscape. Does this disuse suggest that we no longer consider coveting a sin? Is it because we have substituted a more benign word, e.g., envy? Or is it because the Tenth Commandment is no longer applicable since we don't own slaves or donkeys and now consider wives persons rather than property?

The first nine commandments command/prohibit specific behaviors—overt behaviors that can be observed. The Tenth (coveting) prohibits an attitude—a predisposition to feel or act in a certain way. Covert attitudes are more difficult to change than overt behavior. We can decide, for example, that we are going to be nice to some troublesome neighbors and carry through with it. But how do we deal with our secret wish that they would move away?

Coveting has many definitions or faces. One of these, according to the dictionary, is to wish for something earnestly. By earnestly we mean strongly, with great emotion. But what if the thing wished for is, say, a college degree? Does God view this as coveting? Is this what God intended to prohibit? Consider the person who says, "I covet your prayers," or, "I covet our time together." Do these covets run afoul of the Tenth? The dictionary would suggest a no answer and I would agree.

The dictionary suggests a second definition of the word covet: to desire what belongs to another, inordinately or culpably.

The word inordinately means more than what is normal or acceptable. Culpably describes a manner that warrants blame or condemnation. If we want something inordinately, we want it too much; if we want something culpably, we can be blamed or condemned for coveting it. It is these two words—inordinately and culpably—that bring the definition of coveting into alignment with God's prohibition. If the thing we wish for is the property of another, we are *ipso facto* guilty of coveting.

In chapter 29, *Greed,* I ask why people lie, steal, cheat, murder, covet, and other dishonorable, forbidden acts. My answer, in a word, is greed. Greed is the forerunner of the other sins mentioned above. It comes before and opens the door to all other forbidden behaviors. If I covet my neighbor's wife, I must have adultery in mind. If I covet my neighbor's possessions, I must have thievery in mind. All sorts of malice and wrong doing follow greed; one of these is coveting. Because of our greed, we covet, a sin which God detests. Because we covet, we do all sorts of bad things to get what we covet. It's ironic, but we usually are not aware of all the things we covet until advertisers tell us how important it is for us to have them.

It is not considered sinful to want to succeed in our profession, to own a nice house, etc., but when we become obsessed with these things it can become coveting, When getting these things becomes the most important goal of our life, and we are willing to do any thing to get them, coveting becomes idolatry.

God's reasons for condemning covetousness are good and logical. Basic to God's reasoning is the fact that covetousness is a love of self. Our inordinate desires to clothe, feed, and entertain ourselves in ways that "keep up with the Jones" can easily distract us from what is meaningful in life. When keeping up with the Jones is so important that we will do anything to succeed, coveting becomes idolatry. Coveting is an insidious and pervasive sin that can cripple us spiritually; when we cannot keep up with the Jones, we often turn to resentment of them.

Where do we draw the line between wanting and being content with what we have and wanting and seeking more? The Apostle Paul has an answer for us. He wrote in Philippians 4:11-12 that he knew how to be content whatever the circumstances of his life. He knew what it was to be in need and what it was to have plenty. Whether well fed or hungry, Paul states that he was content. What was his secret? "I can do everything through Him (God) who gives me strength." (v 13). Even if we are able to emulate Paul's level of contentment, we must still provide our answer to the questions Jesus asked in Matthew 16:26: "What good will it be for a man if he gains the whole world, yet forfeits his soul? Or what can a man give in exchange for his soul?"

17

ETERNAL LIFE

"For God so loved the world that He gave his only Son, so that everyone who believes in Him may not perish but have eternal life." John 3:16. (GNB)

Imagine being offered a free vacation in either the mountains or at the seashore. You are equally attracted to both. But you cannot have both; you have to choose one. Choosing between two equally attractive alternatives is always difficult. How do you decide? Does it make a difference?

Now consider this real-life, ever-present, inescapable situation: a decision that makes all the difference in the world. When your physical body dies, your immortal soul (in the form of consciousness), leaves the body destined for either heaven or hell. Depending upon what you assume or believe about heaven and hell, which one would you choose as an eternal home for your soul? You must choose between heaven or hell—there is no other option. Do you consider one better than the other? Again, it is your choice; no one else can choose for you. Jesus wants you to choose heaven, and if you do He has a very simple plan for you to follow to gain salvation for your soul. Choosing heaven is a proactive choice. Paradoxically, you can go to hell by default, because you didn't consciously, purposefully choose heaven.

Theological literature abounds with discussions of what happens when we die. For the moment let us consider what happens when we are born. First of all, consider how original man was made. Genesis 2:7 tells the story. "The Lord God formed the man from the dust of the ground and breathed into his nostrils the breath of life, and the man became a living being, created in the likeness of God." This creation was primarily spiritual, although we can say that our body, in a lesser way, was also created in God's image. The physical body was first created and God breathed a soul into the body as a living place for the soul. Before God's act of creation, our soul did not exist. This, in summary, is how the first man was born.

Our physical body, formed of dust, is mortal; our soul is immortal, formed in the image of God. Our soul can never be destroyed. God is the author, creator, and owner of our soul. No person, however powerful, can either destroy or create another person's soul. That is the providence of God alone.

Now, let us jump forward fourscore and ten years and look at the question of what happens when our body dies. Remember, the body goes back to dust and the soul, no longer having a body to live in, has to go to a new home. Where the soul goes is actually decided before the body dies. Choosing between heaven and hell—between joy and sorrow—is the lot of every living person. We are not always aware of having made a decision since it can be made unconsciously. We might even question the fairness of being accountable for a decision we did not actually make. Remember, our failure to make a decision for Heaven is a decision for hell. Jesus is reaching out for us and if we reach out for Him He will take us by the hand and tell us what we must do. See Chapter 4, *Being Born Again,* and Chapter 53, *Repentance*, for the steps in Jesus' simple plan for salvation of our soul.

Choosing between the mountains or the seashore might easily be decided by the flip of a coin, since both choices are equally attractive. Neither has an advantage over the other. Choosing between Heaven and hell, however, is a decision that has lasting, irrevocable, consequences for us. What is Heaven like; what is hell like? Jesus referred to Heaven as "paradise." (Luke 23:43). The Apostle Paul embellished Heaven in glowing terms when (Paraphrase of 1 Corn 2:9), he declared that the eye has not seen, the ear has not heard, nor the heart conceived what God has prepared for those who love Him. Wow! A word picture of hell is the absence of these God-designed qualities; hell is the absence of or separation from God.

Dante's *Inferno* narrates his imaginary journey through life in which he passes through hell and purgatory before reaching paradise. Inside the wide gates of hell, he sees people being punished for their sins on earth, which he views as Divine Judgment. As the author, he lets his poem have a happy ending for himself.

Luke (16:19-31) paints a word picture of hell from which there is no escape, no happy endings. There was a rich man (Dives), who lived a life of self-indulgence and conspicuous consumption, There was a poor man named Lazarus, who sat at Dives' gate hoping for scraps of food from Dives' table. His best friends were the dogs who licked his body sores. Lazarus died and was taken by angels to the lap of Abraham in Heaven. Then the rich man died and was buried. In hell, in tortured pain, he looked up and saw Lazarus beside Abraham. He called out, "Father Abraham, send Lazarus to dip his finger in water and cool my tongue. I'm in agony in this place." Abraham reminded Dives that he lived a rich life on earth and that Lazarus lived a destitute life. The parable ends with Abraham reminding Dives of his sins of omission on earth. It was not what Dives did that got him into hell; it was what he did not do. He simply ignored Lazarus. Besides, Abraham concluded, "There is a great chasm between us and you. No one can cross over from us to you nor can anyone cross over from you to us."

Dives went to hell because of what he did not do. He did not choose to follow Jesus.

18

FAITH

". . . . When you pray and ask for something believe you have already received it, and you will be given whatever you ask for." Mk 11:24. (GNB)

Once upon a time in a land called Oz, there lived an all—seeing and powerful wizard. We all know the story . . . . The wizard did not really have any magical powers but the people chose to believe him anyway. This fact alone gave him more power than any magic potion ever could. He convinced the scarecrow that he had a brain all along, the tin man that he was not lacking a heart, and the lion that he had always had courage. Because they believed, the wizard was able to transform their lives.

It is a story of faith. A true story? No. A true-to-life story? Yes, in the sense that it illustrates how faith in God works in the lives of people.

Faith in God, as the crowning object of our spiritual striving, is a complex sentiment involving elements of experience, knowledge, emotion, and the will. As such, it demands a total person response, involving both head and heart. Whatever the circumstances of our faith, it is a blend or composite of all the elements in our intellectual and psychological being, and is seldom arrived at by only one path. Disciplined study can increase our knowledge of God, but we can never know God through study alone—God has to be experienced.

My faith did not come to me overnight. There was no Damascus Road experience; there was no "Gee Whiz, I've got it!" moment. It had its beginnings in childhood, as I recall, as little more than reflective expressions of what I had been taught by my parents and Sunday school teachers. There was no intellectual understanding of what I said I believed, nor was there any commitment or attachment to it. That was not faith.

As I grew into my stage of adolescent revolt, I felt the pangs of doubt as I began to question the improbabilities of God. I cherished my child-like faith but felt insecure at the thought of it being ill-founded. Still, I wanted to move past my illusion of faith to the reality of faith. This reality could be achieved, I concluded, only by reasoning my way to a pragmatic belief in God. It was a tortuous time for me as I sought some proof of God's existence—the kind of proof that would remove doubt and make believing easier.

What I found was my own answer to the ages-old question of whether anyone is ever convinced by reasoning or scientific inquiry alone of the existence of God. Reasoning can support or buttress our faith, but it cannot lead us to faith. Experience is the litmus test of faith. Any experience of God calls, first, for an emotional response. Intellectual processes can then be used to help us understand what was experienced. Critical to this experiencing process, in addition to emotions and understanding, is the broad question of our will—our decision to believe.

Is faith the same as belief? And how do these two constructs differ from knowing? Current usage of these terms suggests some semantic distinctions. I believe that the Great Wall of China exists even though I have never seen it; the pictorial evidence is convincing. I believe in the law of gravity because I, too, have had an apple fall on my head. In these instances, my belief is based upon knowledge and experience. I have reasons to believe the Atlanta Braves will win the World Series. In a like manner, I can offer reasons for believing that the stock market will turn bullish or bearish. In these instances, my belief is based upon my knowledge of the attending circumstances, intuition, and past experience.

I believe in God. What evidence can I offer in justification of my belief? If we "know" that God exists, even though we have never seen Him, believing would require nothing more than giving assent to that fact. However, believing or having faith in something we cannot prove requires far more conscious commitment. We tend to speak of having faith in those things we cannot prove. Faith signifies a greater investment of the self than does belief. Our need to validate our faith in God rests upon two pillars: the experiential and the pragmatic. Of crucial importance is which of them we make the foundation stone in our quest to know Jesus as our personal Savior. In my own case, it was and remains a matter of experiencing God through revelation. This is the foundation of my belief, and I suspect it is true of all believers. It is far less likely that we would reason a belief that God exists, and then accept Him as our Savior. Rather, we use reason to support our faith which is necessarily born out of our experience of God. If God exists will He reward believers and punish non-believers? Consider the following statements about belief in God and the consequences of each choice:

1. If we believe and we are right, we gain eternal life.
2. If we believe and we are wrong, nothing is lost.
3. If we do not believe and we're right, nothing is gained.
4. If we do not believe and we're wrong. we gain eternal damnation.

Given thee consequences of believing and not believing, the rational, prudent person will choose to believe, even though there is no intellectual understanding of the truth of his belief. Neither is there a conviction of the importance of his belief. Lacking any experience of God, as revealed in the Bible, there is no personal interest in the truth. Without any emotional assent or attachment to their belief, it lacks the property of embracing Christ as Savior and Lord. Faith in God begins with and is manifested in the psycho-spiritual needs and strivings of people. Faith is a more complex dimension of the religious sentiment than is believing or knowing.

Our need to validate our faith in God rests upon two pillars: the experiential and the pragmatic. Of crucial importance is which of them we make the foundation stone in our quest to know Jesus as our personal Savior. In my case, it was and remains a matter of experiencing God through revelation. This is the foundation of my belief and I suspect it is true of all believers. It is far less likely that we would reason a belief that God exists and then accept Him as savior. Rather, we use reason to support our faith which is necessarily born out of our experience of God.

For people who believe in God, no explanation of His existence is necessary; for those who do not believe, no explanation is adequate.

19

FEAR

"There is no fear in love, but perfect love casts out fear; for fear has to do with punishment, and whoever fears has not reached perfection in love. We love because He first loved us." 1 Jn 4:18-19. (NRSV)

Ask a psychologist about fear and he will explain it as a basic human emotion, one that alerts us to the presence of danger. It prepares our body to fight or flee. A theologian will describe fear as the reverential awe of believers toward God. The difference is that, historically, two semantical meanings have been given to the same word. Each meaning, in context, can be defended without contradicting the other. Moreover, fear, at it's core, is a faith issue because it is the opposite of faith, especially in the religious domain.

Throughout the Jewish scriptures we read that "the fear of God is the beginning of understanding . . . wisdom . . . knowledge." In fact, the fear of God is a recurring theme throughout the Old Testament. The Psalms, for example, are full of admonitions: "No wonder you are greatly feared! Who can stand before you when your anger explodes?" (Ps.76:7). "The nations will fear the name of the Lord, and all the kings of the earth your glory." (Ps. 102:15). The moral of these verses is that until we understand who God is and develop a reverential fear of Him, we cannot have true wisdom. This comes only from understanding who God is and that He is holy, just, and righteous. God is further complimented as eternal, all knowing, and all powerful. And, oh yes, God is love. He is truly an awesome God. Wow!

In human relationships fear and love are incompatible. This cultural mind-set complicates our understanding of the preachment to both love and fear God at the same time. "How can I do this?" we might ask. "How can I both love and fear God at the same time? Do I have to choose? Is the conflict I am feeling real or is it something that can be resolved or explained? Is it a problem of semantics for me?"

Love is the very nature of God; it is the essence of His being. He creates us in love; He rules us in love, and judges us in love. God cannot be otherwise. Love is the one word that describes all that God is. Why, we ponder, must we fear God who is perfect in love?

In Biblical usage the word fear is burdened by two different interpretations. The first is a softened meaning which conveys reverential awe of God. This is the meaning taken by believers: persons who love God. The second reflects the idea of being scared of God, God is seen as being arbitrary, vindictive, unloving, and uncaring. This meaning is the understanding of the non-believer. The believer loves God, having moved past fear. The non-believer has not yet experienced the love of God, he is controlled by fear.

It is embarrassing to remember that we all were once non-believers. We did not disbelieve, we simply had not yet felt the claim that God has on our lives. As God revealed Himself to us we rejoiced in the intimacy, closeness, and safety that He offers us as believers. It was at this point that we surrendered and revelled in the unconditional love of God. We outgrew the fear that we once had of God. John, the Evangelist, supports this growth process by writing: " . . . perfect love casts out fear." (1 Jn 14:18). Fear goes; love stays. Henri J.M. Nouwen opines that we cannot love God as long as we are afraid of Him. (*Bread for the Journey*. 1996). He further argues that

Jesus came into the world to help us overcome our fear of God.

Can we love God without first fearing Him? It is fruitless to pursue this question; the important question is, "Do we love God?" If we as Christians love God, people will see God in us by looking at our lives and the way we act toward them. If we fear God, others will see a different us.

20

FOOLISHNESS

"For we ourselves were once foolish, disobedient, and wrong. We were slaves to passions and pleasures of all kinds. We spent our lives in malice and envy; others hated us and we hated them. But when the kindness and love of God was revealed, He saved us."
Tit 3:3-5a. (GNB)

In spite of ridicule and criticisms from his contemporaries, Thomas Edison doggedly pursued his goal of finding a suitable material for use as the filament in the incandescent light bulb. He was thought of as being unrealistic and foolish. To his critics he was foolish because he was wasting his time on a gadget of questionable use and value; what he was doing did not make good sense. Without a predictable payoff it was a foolish undertaking. Still, he persisted, explaining that he knew 5,000 things that would not work.

To them there was no payoff. Fortunately, Edison pursued and achieved his goal. What was viewed as foolishness to his critics was thought perfectly rational by Edison.

Decisions about the foolishness or acceptance of any behavior must begin with a consideration of the goal at hand. Waving a loaded gun at one's head would most certainly be described as dangerous and foolish. Would this description apply if the person with the gun were considering suicide? Goals can be chosen rationally as a response to a perceived need, but decision making about goals always involve degrees of uncertainty and risk since it is concerned with the future. Such was the case of the Teacher (was it Solomon?) in Ecclesiastes. He sought power only to find it was corrupting. He sought riches only to find that the poor slept better at night than he did. He sought knowledge only to find that smart people do stupid things. Subjectively, his goals seemed rational, and he was successful in achieving them only to find that they did not satisfy his need. He concluded that all was vanity. Where did he go wrong?

Maybe the answer can be found in the case of a patient of mine who exemplified the Prodigal Son (Lk 15:11-32). After high school he chose not to go college. He wanted the excitement that partying and the night-life scene offered. Freedom, relationships without commitments, and being seen as cool drove him on. Only marginally employed he soon fell in with the "wrong" crowd and numerous wrong turns in his life caused the bright lights of his self-centered hopes to dim. Much like the vanity cries of the Teacher the patient concluded that all the goals and values he had tried to live his life by were wrong. "Look at me!" he cried, "I'm alone, lonely, and don't know where to turn." Tragic, we might feel. Foolish and unacceptable, we might conclude, because his decisions were contrary to both education and experience. They were ill—conceived and nonrational.

Do we make decisions in the spiritual domain of our lives the same way we do in the secular? Consider the following line of reasoning, often referred to as Pascal's Wager. If we believe in God and God does exist we gain eternal salvation. If we believe in God and we are wrong we have not gained or lost anything. If we choose not to believe in God and we are right, again, we haven't gained or lost anything. But if we choose not to believe and God does, in fact, exist we suffer damnation. Using this line of reasoning, do we choose to believe in God because it is the safest thing to do, offering us the greatest benefit and the least risk?

The problem with seeking to make a safe bet or wager in order to gain entrance to heaven assumes God does not mind how we come to Him. God's desire and plan for us to come to Him has been made perfectly clear. We must come by faith in Jesus; we must grow in faith, live by faith, and spread the faith. Believing that we can gain salvation through the analytical process of pragmatic decision making is foolishness!

21

FORGIVENESS

"If he (your brother) sins against you seven times in one day, and each time he comes to you saying, 'I repent,' you must forgive him." Lk 17:4. (GNB)

"Forgive him?" After what he did to me? You must be joking."

Just the word "forgive" can trigger all kinds of intense feelings, from resentment and judgment to anger and rage. Forgiving, at first glance, does seem unnatural. Our laws, our sense of justice and fair play all tell us that wrongdoers must be punished. They must pay for the hurt and pain they cause others. Believing this way, we respond with anger, hatred, and thoughts of revenge. We may realize in our hearts that forgiveness is a more noble and Christian response but we find it hard to practice in our daily lives.

But imagine a society that values and supports vindictiveness and retaliation.

Imagine the consequences of any society living by the rule of "an eye for an eye and a tooth for a tooth." It would be, as one wag has suggested, a society of blind, toothless people.

Now contrast that scenario to God's plan for His people. Its hallmarks are peace and harmony; its core is forgiveness—the opposite of conflict and retaliation. Jesus taught that as members of the family of God we must abandon our desire for revenge and, instead, live by the rule of forgiveness. His teaching challenges our basic instinct to strike back at those who hurt us. If we don't strike back, we argue, we will be hurt again.

Does living by the rule of forgiveness make us wimps? Does it turn us into doormats? No. Any unknowing person can carry a grudge and determine to get even. When we see people behaving that way we naturally conclude that it is the only way they can behave—that is their only option. That's what unknowing people do. But Christians have choices, and choosing to live by the rule of forgiveness reflects strength, not weakness. Forgiveness is sometimes forced upon people by attending circumstances, but such forgiveness does not come from the heart; it is neither freely nor sincerely given. People who submit to these circumstances are outer directed. Christians, on the other hand, forgive because they know and trust the will of God. They have inculcated Jesus' teaching into an overall attitude of forgiveness. They are inner—directed people and practice forgiveness out of choice.

From both a spiritual and a psychological point of view forgiveness simply makes good sense. No one wants to live with anger, resentment, guilt, etc. Forgiveness frees us from being a victim of our own anger and hate. Forgiveness is the means of mending broken relationships. It cleanses our heart and mind and restores an innocence that makes us free to love again.

People who keep anger and hate alive, nurturing it for whatever purpose they have, rob themselves of energy and attention that could be used for constructive purposes. When we try to keep the socially unacceptable feelings of hate and anger hidden for fear of embarrassment or criticism, the psychological costs of protecting our negative feelings are great. In financial terms, it is an imprudent expenditure of psychological energy—a poor investment. Further, hanging on to our anger and hate can adversely affect our immune system making us susceptible to a wide gambit of psychological and physical ills. We forgive for our benefit, just as we forgive for the benefit of others. When we understand this we can begin to practice love and acceptance rather than judgment and revenge. When we replace our negative feelings with love and forgiveness we can improve the quality of our lives and relationships.

Some people complain that they tried to forgive someone and found they couldn't. They tried, they say, but were unsuccessful. Forgiveness is difficult; it comes naturally only with prayer and practice. A critical factor in determining the ease or difficulty of forgiving is the nature of the offense. How grievous was it? Was it intended? Was it repeated? Was there any remorse? This was the story of Corrie Ten Boom. After her liberation from a Nazi concentration camp at the end of World War II she was confronted by a former camp guard who asked for her forgiveness. As hard as she tried, she was unable to forgive him. Apparently the memories of the horrors and indignities she suffered in the camp were so grievous she could not release her anger and resentment. She prayed, "Jesus, I can't forgive this man, forgive me." Wondrously, she later reported, she felt a sense of immediate forgiveness. She was able to release the guard from his past and to release herself from her past.

But difficulties encountered in giving up feelings of hate and anger toward someone who has hurt us or someone we love are not always directly related to the severity of the offense. Some people can forgive a betrayal or an abuse as easily as others might forgive a slight or an annoyance. Some people are so thin-skinned they are offended by the most insignificant, unintended misdeed. Others seem to have an immunity against even the most severe offenses.

Forgiving is also complicated by a superficial understanding of what is involved. Deciding to forgive is a necessary but insufficient condition for true forgiveness. The decision has to be incorporated into an overall attitude of forgiveness which hopefully transforms itself into forgiveness as a way of life. When we reach this level of Christian maturity we simply become forgiving people. We don't debate whether to forgive or not, we just forgive. We are programmed or hard wired to forgive, so to speak.

It is not necessary that we actually communicate our forgiveness to our offender. No words have to be spoken, no letters have to written, although this can be an important part of the forgiving and healing process. Whether we actually confront our offender or write a note, we must behave toward that person so our change of heart can be noticed. This is the critical requirement: emptying our heart and mind of all negative feelings toward our offender. We must be able to say, "I forgive you. Yes, I remember what you did but I now understand why you did what you did. I have only love for you."

Forgiveness is not approving or condoning the punishing behavior of an offender. If we had to accept the objectionable behavior then forgiveness would be impossible. Neither is forgiveness simply pretending that everything is alright. The difference between forgiving and pretending everything is O. K. can be very deceptive, providing a false basis for rebuilding a broken relationship. Genuine forgiveness, moreover, is impossible if our original anger and hate are denied or repressed. Finally, as Christians, we must be careful not to let our forgiving give us a sense of moral superiority or self-righteousness. If we forgive others because of feelings of sympathy or because we view them as incapable of upright behavior we are in danger of confusing forgiveness with judgment.

If an orange is squeezed orange juice comes out. Why is this? Because that is what is inside an orange. What comes out when we are squeezed (offended)? We have reached a high level of Christian maturity when nothing but love and forgiveness come out. Love and forgiveness come out because that is what's inside us. Forgiving is what Jesus expects us to do. Obeying Him makes us Christlike.

22

FORTITUDE

*"My fellow believers, be careful
that no one among us has a heart so
evil and unbelieving that he will turn
away from the living Christ . . . .
For we are all partners with Christ if
we hold firmly to the end the confidence
we had at the beginning."*
Heb 3:12 & 14. (GNB)

Let us begin with a fantasy. Do not ask
how we will do this—that would destroy the
fantasy. Imagine that we are privileged to
visit a Museum of Heroes and Saints. The door
is open and there is no admission charge.
Still, we pause before entering. Should we
remove our shoes? We recall how God appeared
to Moses in the form of a burning bush (Ex
3:5). "Don't come any closer Moses. Take off
your sandals, for you are standing on holy
ground."

Observing the felt need for solemnity and decorum, we enter. Converging in a large rotunda are many connecting halls and corridors. To our left there is a Hall of Heroes. Here, we see the images of George Washington, Thomas Edison, Lewis Pasteur among others. WoW! To our right there is the Sanctuary of Saints. Prominent among the many likenesses here are Abraham, Moses, David, Paul, Martin Luther, John Calvin, and John Wesley. Wow!

How were these greats selected for inclusion? What were the criteria? Were the criteria different for heroes and saints? What made them different? What was their secret? Their strength?

The common thread in the lives of all of them, both heroes and saints, is that fortitude is an essential quality of character in both spiritual and secular undertakings. They were willing to be led by God. They had the courage of their convictions. They were willing to endure all things. They stood firm in their faith—a faith that was their strength—a strength that was a composite of perseverance and the idea of social good. Fortitude is never a stand alone virtue; it is fused with social and spiritual value.

Consider the stories of Thomas Edison and Moses, two of the greats the Museum, While developing the filament for the incandescent light bulb, Thomas Edison experimented with

5,000 materials, none of which worked. Was he discouraged? No. "I know 5,000 things that don't work." he said optimistically. As God's appointed agent, Moses led the Hebrews through trial after trial as they journeyed from Egypt to Canaan, the land that God promised them. He helped them find their way past starvation, sickness, impatience, and despair.

It is not easy to be a Christian; it is not easy to truly follow Jesus. Fortitude must strengthen us every step of our spiritual journey. It must also characterize our prayer life. When we put our hand to the plow—to be a follower of Jesus—we must remain steadfast, no regrets, no second thoughts, no looking back. God is looking for and needs followers who have the fortitude to rise above all the negatives in life and pursue the positives.

In his writing about the four cardinal virtues (prudence, temperance, justice, and fortitude*), C.S. Lewis (*Mere Christianity.* 1943) states that fortitude includes two kinds of courage—the kind that faces danger and the kind that "sticks with it" under pain. He concludes that we cannot practice any of the other virtues without bringing fortitude into play. There is also the implication that fortitude must be guided by prudence and a willingness to endure any hardships and difficulties that may come. Without prudence—

our desire to know God and do what is right—fortitude serves no meaningful purpose. Fortitude is not truly a virtue unless it is directed to some ultimate good.

Earlier I wrote that it is not easy being a Christian. Let me put it differently: it is easy to fall from our faith. It is easy to forget the excitement and joy we felt when we first accepted Jesus. Temptations, fears, and hard decisions confront us. Living our faith is sometimes contrary to what society tells us is right. Sometimes we have to make sacrifices and compromises to be faithful to God and His Commandments. When these hard times come we must not rely on our own strength. We have God's assurance that He will walk with us on our journey through life. The Apostle Paul felt this assurance when he wrote to Timothy "I have fought the good fight, I have finished the race, I have kept the faith." (2 Tim 4:7)

When the going gets tough in our lives there is no better way to prepare than to pray "Lord. give me guts."

-* In the accepted scheme there are four cardinal virtues and three theological virtues. The latter three are faith, hope, and charity

23

FULFILLMENT

"When I was a child, my speech, feelings, and thinking were those of a child; now that I am a man I have no more use for childish ways."
1 Cor 13:11. (GNB)

"In the bulb there is a flower, in the seed, an apple tree; in cocoons, a hidden promise: butterflies will soon be free!"

These lines from the hymn *of Promise* mirror the drama of God's intentions and expectations of all His creations. It reflects the drama of growth along a continuum from potential to fulfillment, a growth process that is programmed into all living creatures. The words "hard wired" help us to understand that there is a plan or purpose that differentiates one creature or being from all others. My blueberry plants predictably produce berries when properly cared for in a hospitable environment. They have no free will—they can't produce anything other than what God programmed them to produce. Fulfillment for them is producing berries in season.

A young baby is the most dependent of all God's creatures. He depends upon care givers (parents, hopefully) to provide all his needs. He is driven by a survival instinct and lets care givers know when his needs are not being met. As a child matures he progresses into a counter-dependent mode of relating in which he wants to do things his way, when he wants to. This was a challenging period for my wife and me. I can remember how my son insisted he could tie his own shoes even as I urged him to let me do it. "Patience, Russ." my wife would say as I waited. Wanting to do things for themselves is a necessary first step for children toward the long-term goal of fulfillment: becoming a socialized adult. Unfortunately, society holds up independence as the ultimate goal in a person's life. No one is independent in the final sense; we are all dependent on each other. Recognizing and accepting our inter-dependence is one hallmark of a fulfilled person.

Abraham Maslow (*Motivation and Personality*. 1954) has provided us a meaningful guide to measure progress toward fulfillment. Presented as a hierarchy, the most basic need is our bodily needs. Stories of hunger throughout the world tell us that some people never really

Russ Holloman, Ph.D.

satisfy this need. Persons who do satisfy
this need want to know that the means of
satisfying it are safe, i.e., having a secure
income. Implied in the hierarchy is the idea
that once a lower level need is satisfied the
next higher need becomes operative. Next
above the safety needs are our needs for
love and acceptance—social needs. They are
followed by our needs for esteem, to have
a good reputation and feel we are accepted.
At the top of the hierarchy is our need for
actualization, the need to become what we are
capable of becoming. The actualized person is
a fulfilled person.

In one of his formulations Maslow placed our
spiritual needs at the top, arguing that our
spiritual life is the basic component of our
biological life. It is easy to follow Maslow
and visualize an actualized, fulfilled person
as a mature Christian. Why can't everyone
ascend to the peak of the hierarchy? In my
many years of practicing psychotherapy, I
continually searched for answers to this
question as I worked with patients whose
growth was stalled at a lower level in
the hierarchy. I found a lot of erroneous
thinking among these patients about the idea
of fulfillment. They saw fulfillment (I always
used the term success) as the result of
education, hard work, driving ambition, and
delayed satisfaction; preconditions they were

reluctant to buy into. Always, I presented success as an attitude rather than a litany of achievements.

One of the most encompassing and enduring definitions of success differs markedly from our contemporary definition. Variously attributed to different authors, one widely-accepted version reads: "To live well, to laugh often, to love much, to gain the respect of intelligent people, to win the love of little children. To fill one's niche and accomplish one's task. To leave the world better than one finds it whether by an improved flower, a perfect poem, or another life ennobled. To never lack appreciation of earth's beauty or fail to express it, to always look for the best in others, to give the best one has. To make one's life an inspiration and one's memory a benediction. This is success."

This is fulfillment! God would say, "Amen."

24

GENTLENESS

"Take my yoke upon you, and learn from me; for I am gentle and humble in heart, and you will find rest for your souls." (Mt 11:29).

"As God's chosen ones, holy and beloved, clothe yourself with compassion, kindness, meekness, and patience." (Col 3:12). (NRSV)

Imagine a mountain stream flowing quietly toward the sea. In its path large rocks protrude from the stream bed, interrupting the smooth flow of the water. But as the soft water flows against the hard rocks, it gradually erodes their shape and size. Wow! The effect of the water flowing past the rocks comes close to the Biblical teaching about the strength of gentleness. Which is stronger, the water or the rocks?

Gentleness is not weakness; it is strength. Gentle people are strong because they are able to remain calm and composed in the face of stress. Gentleness is an active state of being, describing how we should treat others; it is a quality that comes from the heart and the soul. It is an attitude, a value, a predisposition to respect others in all our relationships. Gentleness flows from agape (God's love) and is rooted in goodwill toward others. Gentleness is related to meekness; and they are so similar in meaning they are often used interchangeably. Moveover, in some dictionaries, each is used in the definition of the other.

If gentleness describes our Christian way of relating to others, meekness can be described as our Christian response when others try to take advantage of us or do not know how to respond to our gentleness. The Golden Rule and Jesus' teaching about forgiveness both apply here. Be gentle toward others and forgive them when they don't respond in like manner. We can't control how others behave toward us but we are free to choose how we will both approach and respond to others. Both gentleness and meekness are born of strength, not weakness. Gentleness and meekness are hallmarks of the Christian way.

It is seemingly difficult to find a hospitable, rewarding environment for gentleness in today's society (circa 2011). There is a marked chasm between the ideal of gentleness/meekness and the societal norm of interpersonal relationships, particularly in the public arena. A win-at-all-costs attitude doesn't provide a fertile ground for gentleness to grow and spread. Unbounded competition inevitably results in adversarial relations more akin to Social Darwinism (survival of the fittest), than to the prescription of Biblical gentleness. Unfortunately, albeit tragically, gentleness/meekness has become synonymous with weakness, lack of courage, and an unwillingness to contest violations of personal rights.

The word gentleness often conjures up a mental picture of the 97-pound weakling of the Charles Atlas body-building promotions. Weaklings have to be gentle and submissive, we reason, they have no choice. On the other hand, we are duly impressed when the physically strong show gentleness, helping us to understand that gentleness is more related to strength of character than to physical strength. Consider the strength and gentleness shown by Jesus, Lincoln, Gandhi, Einstein, and Mother Teresa. The gentleness of these persons was their strength: a strength drawn from and matured in God.

James (3:13-18) writes about the gentleness of wisdom. There is also much to gain when we consider the wisdom of gentleness. Max Lacudo found this wisdom and chose gentleness when he wrote in *When God Whispers Your Name.* (1995)

"Nothing is won by force, I choose to be gentle.

If I raise my voice may it be only in praise.

If I clinch my fist, may it be only in prayer.

If I make a demand, may it be only of myself."

We must become meek in both spirit and demeanor to faithfully live by the word of God. This same meekness is a prerequisite for sharing the Word with others. The spirit of God manifests itself only when and where there is an attitude of love and meekness. Gentleness does not come naturally, it must be learned. valued, and practiced. Gentleness is Godly and God expects us to be gentle, as He is gentle.

25

GIVING

"Give, and it will be given to you. A good measure, pressed down, shaken together, running over, will be put into your lap; for the measure you give will be the measure you get back." Lk.6:38. (NRSV)

Who, as a child, was not told time and again that it was better to give than to receive? As children we might have thought that it applied only to birthdays, Christmas, and, possibly, Valentine's Day. Ask a young child whether it is more fun (blessed) to give or receive presents at Christmas, and the answer will always be the same. It is difficult for children and many adults to understand the benefits of giving when there is no receiving: when there is no give and take, no exchange, when it is all one way. Growing up in a world that promotes and supports self-interest by looking out for number one hinders our understanding and acceptance of the preachment that it is better to give than receive.

The benefits of receiving are obvious, but are there any benefits to the giver? Is it more blessed to give than to receive? Yes. Consider the case of Ebenezer Scrooge, the lonely, unhappy, cantankerous, miserable old man in Dicken's *A Christmas Carol*.

He was accustomed to accumulating wealth; giving was a foreign, unacceptable idea to him. However, a Christmas Eve experience changed him into a generous, kind, and caring person. He discovered the truth that had eluded him for his many years: happiness comes from giving, not receiving.

Solomon's life (Read Ecclesiastes and 1 Kings, *Holy Bible*) was not as favorable as Scrooge's. He believed the key to happiness and success in life was to accumulate power, wisdom, riches, and pleasure. He became, indeed, one of the wisest, richest men who ever lived. So, how did he feel about his wealth? "Vanity, all is vanity." was his conclusion. Solomon never experienced that moment when he could say, "This is good, let it last."

The blessings of giving to charity are accepted on faith, and we can cite many different reasons why we give, particularly to our church. There is the traditional idea that giving to our church is an expression of gratitude and love of God, especially when we remember that every thing we have belongs to God. Churches and other voluntary organizations depend upon giving; they have no other way to raise money. The services they provide benefit all of society. Unlike economic organizations, churches are fused with value. They take on an institutional nature. What would our society be like if there were no churches, no Red Cross, no March of Dimes? The good they do is so great—so irreplaceable—we cannot let them fail. Whether we give to God or to the Red Cross, our motivation is spiritual. Our giving is God-centered, in the spirit of humility and love. Our giving will be blessed when we give for the right reasons. If we give for recognition or approval from others, that is all the reward we will ever receive.

"What shall I offer the Lord for all he has done for me?" the Psalmist asked (Ps. 116:12). God does not ask for repayment of His gifts to us, but since we give gifts to friends as tokens of appreciation, should not we also ask the Psalmist's question? Giving out of gratitude and love—giving from the heart—pleases God. It also involves a greater measure of self-giving. Giving because we feel obligated fails this test.

There is a oft told story about a poor man explaining to a neighbor how he was given a new (to him) car. "A friend gave it to me." he said. "I wish I had a friend like that." quipped the neighbor. The poor man replied, "I wish I could be that kind of friend." Which man best understood the blessing of giving?

Surprisingly, ongoing research is revealing that voluntary giving also benefits us psychologically and physiologically. Professor Arthur C. Brooks (*Giving Makes You Rich*, 2007) found that giving affects our brain chemistry in positive ways. Often, for example, feelings of euphoria are reported by people after acts of giving. Giving also lowers the stress hormones that cause unhappiness. People who give also report they feel more connected with other individuals and with the community. The bottom line of Professor Brooks' research on giving is that it is not just good for our favorite causes, it is also good for us.

Ted Turner, the flamboyant multi-billionaire, once shared that over a period of three years he gave away over half of what he had. "To be honest, my hand shook as I signed it away." he said. "I knew I was taking myself out of the race to be the richest man in the world." As Mr. Turner was perhaps thinking, the single most powerful way to succeed in life is have more love and concern for others. He experienced the joy of giving.

26

GOODNESS

> *"For this reason you must make every effort to support your faith with goodness, and your goodness with knowledge, and knowledge with self-control, and self-control with endurance, and endurance with godliness, and godliness with mutual affection, and affection with love.* (2 Pet 1:5-7). (NRSV)

If I were to describe our family sedan as a good car, would you know exactly what I meant? Is it dependable? Does it require little maintenance? Is it comfortable? Is it economical? My one-word description of the car as "good" does not answer any of these questions. The word, good, can indeed, have many meanings. You could be sure of my meaning only if you knew the context I was referring to.

Whether as a noun or an adjective, good gets meaning from its context; it cannot stand alone. It must be complemented. When we describe something as good, we usually mean it is good for some purpose. A hoe is good for weeding the garden. For sure, a hoe is better than a shovel for weeding. A shovel, on the other hand, is good for digging. Both the hoe and the shovel are judged as good only when used for particular purposes.

Good is a word that invites and depends upon other words to give it meaning. When used alone, it leaves us waiting for " . . . for what." Such is its nature. Most dictionaries go to great length to cover all the possible contexts. Consider "Good as gold," and "Good for nothing." Gold implies a standard of metallic purity. "Good for nothing" suggests something is without value or purpose—no good can come from it.

What is good? Strictly speaking, only God is good. Mark's gospel (10:17-18) makes this point: "As He (Jesus) was starting on a journey, a stranger ran up and kneeling before him asked,'Good Master, what must I do to win eternal life?' Jesus answered him, "Why do you call Me good? No one is good except God alone."

How, then, is God good? First, His works of creation are good. When God surveyed what He had created, He paused and said." "It is good.

It is very good." All God's works are good. God's gifts to us are good. He gives us the beauty of His creation, the goodness of rain, sun, the variety and taste of food—His gifts are endless. Most importantly, He gave us a Savior. He gives these gifts whether we love Him or not—whether we are good or not. That is goodness beyond comparison, and God's laws are good. Paul attested, "Therefore the law is in its self holy and the commandment is holy and just and good." (Rom 7:12) The goodness of God's character is revealed in His relations with us. He is just (Ia 30:18), He is forgiving (1 John 1:9), and He is faithful (Deut 7:9).

Only God is good. The rest of us are good only by God's standard of goodness. Goodness is defined in terms of God, not God in terms of goodness.

Who can be good as God is good? Judged by God's standard, no body. Still, Jesus in His sermon on the mount commanded: "You, like the lamp, must shed your light among your fellows, so that, when they see the good you do, they may give praise to your Father in heaven." (Mt 5:16)

A psychological theory, referred to as Heider's balance theory, suggests that humans have an unconscious need to keep their relations with others balanced. If someone does us a favor we look for ways to return the favor. Returning the favor keeps the relationship balanced. This need for balance was perhaps the motive when some followers asked Jesus, "What must we do to perform the work of God?" (Jn 6:28) Jesus replied, "This is the work of God: that you believe in Him whom He sent." (v.29)

We learned in Sunday School that we cannot win God's favor by good works alone. We are justified by faith. We believe in and love God and want to serve Him by acts of charity and compassion for others. James (Ja 1:22) helps us to resolve our quandary by writing, "But be doers of the word, and not merely hearers who deceive themselves."

As believers we want to be doers of the good works. As we seek guidance of the Holy Spirit we will begin to imitate the goodness of God. We will look for ways to help others; we will become more generous, more loving, and more forgiving. We will become more intentional, more relevant. Gradually, we clothe ourselves with the attitude of believing and doing.

Good works (gifts to God) are expressed in all love relationships, whether to God, our families, or our neighbors. Because we love we want to do good toward them. All good works must always be performed from a pure motive derived from the power of God.

27

GRACE

". . . . God's grace is so abundant. and His love for us is so great, that while we were spiritually dead in our disobedience, He brought us to life with Christ. It is by God's grace that you have been saved." Eph 2:4-5 (GNB)

Two walls of my office are decorated with a diverse collection of framed quotations, Bible verses, photos, etc. Most of them were gifts and there is a story behind each. The messages they present range from Biblical quotations to psychological and philosophical principles. Two of them are positioned close together because their message is complementary; they are two sides of the same coin. One, a needlepoint, reads: "God's grace is getting what we don't deserve." The second is a picture of an Easter scene depicting an empty tomb. The printed message

114

is a paraphrase of 1 Corn 15:17: "If Christ was not raised from the dead our faith is in vain." Often. I turn from my study, lean back in my chair, and contemplate the shared truth of these two messages. Two words stand out: grace and faith. And I am quickly led to Paul's preachment that we are justified by faith (Rm 1:17). God's grace makes this possible, making faith the key to salvation. His grace is central to our understanding and practice of Christian faith and life; it is basic to our faith.

Grace is a beautiful word because it is given by God.

All of God's qualities are reflected in His grace: His love, His righteousness, His holiness, His truth, His justice, and His mercy. I know of no one word, with the exception of love, that captures the essence of God's Amazing Grace. While we can easily and confidently declare that God is the source of grace, we are confounded in our efforts to explain just what it is. Simply put, God's grace is His unmerited favor toward us. It is a gift, freely given. It is an unmerited gift, given without any expectation of return. There is nothing we can do to merit God's love, forgiveness, and grace. It is His desire, His power, and His willingness to do for us what we cannot do for ourselves. Since grace is central to our understanding and practice of Christian faith and life, it follows that we individually experience grace in some unique ways. Despite any differences in our receiving and expressing God's grace, it has two important implications for us. One, there is no room for self-righteousness. We are all sinners. There is no basis for thinking of ourselves as being deserving, or that we are better than others. There is no room for pretense or delusion.

The second implication is that grace is not obtained by compliance with specified rules or rituals. Nor does grace obtain by our not doing forbidden things. There is no way we can claim to have earned grace.

John Wesley, founder of the Methodist Church, saw grace in three sequential levels. While he viewed grace as indivisible, he maintained that it precedes salvation as prevenient grace, continues to justification grace, and is brought to fruition in sanctifying grace. Prevenient grace comes to us at the moment of conception or birth. (Prevenient means comes before). It stays in the soul, making it holy. Prevenient grace creates a desire to know God and empowers us to respond to God's invitation to be in relationship with Him. It helps us to discern the difference between good and evil and further helps us to choose good. This grace is always present with us, but it can be refused.

Justifying grace is often associated with what we call conversion or being born again. It points to forgiveness, reconciliation, and pardon. It involves a new beginning, following repentance and conversion. Our relationship with God is restored.

It is tempting to focus on justifying grace since it involves pardon and forgiveness, along with a new peace of joy and love.

But Wesley maintained that we do not end our Christian journey with repentance and forgiveness. It is not a time to sit back and rest. Rather, we are to press on, being sanctified by God's grace, to grow and mature in our ability to live as Jesus lived.

Most Christian communions share a common belief about the core theology of grace. Some agree in whole, others agree in part. All agree that grace is an undeserved, unmerited gift from a loving God.

28

THE GREAT COMMISSION

> *"Go then, to all peoples everywhere
> and make them my disciples: baptize
> them in the name of the Father,
> the Son, and the Holy Spirit, and
> teach them to obey everything I have
> commanded you. And I will be with you
> always, to the very end of the age.*
> Mt 28:19-20 (GNB)

All organizations—churches included—face
the problem of recruiting and keeping new
members. This requirement is particularly
true when the mission or purpose of the
organization is greater then what one person
can do. Business (utilitarian) organizations
hire new employees by paying them a salary.
Coercive (authoritarian) organizations, such
as prisons and draftee armies, can make
people take part whether they want to or not.
A third type of organization, of which the
church is a prime example, can be described

as normative, suggesting that new members are attracted because they value the rewards of belonging. The resulting relationship is moral in nature. Each of the three types presented above are not pure; each has some features of the others. Churches, for example, employ paid staff members.

Christianity (believers and followers of Jesus) began as a sect within the restrictive structures of Judaism. Today the Christian church is the world's largest body of believers. Wow!

This seemingly unbelievable outcome had its beginning with a small group of apostles who accepted Jesus' invitation to "Follow me." They believed and they followed, all the time harboring some doubts. They were an unlikely, motley group. Their time with Jesus was marked with both denials and desertions. But their broken faith was restored when they were confronted by the resurrected Jesus. And when the Holy Spirit came upon them during the festival of Pentecost, they suddenly and dramatically began preaching boldly that the resurrected Jesus was "both Lord and Christ."

The resurrected Jesus commanded the eleven disciples go forth in what is today referred to as the Great Commission. Later, Jesus called Paul and designated him an Apostle to the Gentiles.

(Chapter 9 of Acts tells the miraculous, inspiring story of Paul's conversion on the road to Damascus. Prior to his conversion, Paul had been the chief persecutor of Jesus.)

Assured that Jesus was with them the eleven and Paul began creating small churches throughout a vast geographical empire that was not always sympathetic to the claims and demands of the Gospel they were teaching. They are the heroes of the church. They gave their all; all but one (John) suffered a violent death. Because of their efforts what began as a grassroots movement of Jewish peasants became a powerful institution and dominant force in Western culture. From the dusty roads of first century Palestine to the modern saga of mega-churches our Christian faith has been championed by successive generations of saints who accepted the Commission and went forth. How many times has the baton passed hands?

Recognizing, on the one hand, that Christianity is the worlds largest religion belies the fact, on the other hand, that today 15 per cent of Americans profess no faith at all. As Jesus might say, "The crop is large, who will harvest it?" It is easy and convenient for us to argue that the harvesting is the responsibility of the clergy—is not that what they are paid to do? Is not that what they are trained to do? It would seem out of place for laity to do the pastor's work. Defending this argument against our conscience is not easy. The work of the church (harvesting, etc.) is too big and too important to leave up to the clergy. In my church—Methodist—we have both ordained ministers and lay ministers, so you can see my bias. I have always believed that the secret of church growth is involving the laity in meaningful ministries, growth both in numbers and in a deepening awareness of the Christ's promise of salvation.

Every professed Christian has been given a crucial and non-transferable task to reach out to the world for Jesus Christ. Even though the Commission was given to the Disciples, it is equally applicable to everyone who calls themselves Christian. Our faith is not a private individual matter; it calls us to serve others because of how Christ has affected our lives.

29

GREED

" . . . watch out and guard yourselves from every kind of greed; because your true life is not made up of things you own, no matter how rich you may be." Lk 12:15. (GNB)

Why do people lie, steal, cheat, murder, covet, commit adultery and other dishonorable, forbidden acts? One answer fits all: greed—the self-serving, never-ending desire for money, power, position, influence, pleasure, etc. Greed lurks behind all our wrongdoing and we unknowingly practice greed because of our selfishness. Greed is insidious and pervasive; it can rightly be called the mother of all sins. It is the wellspring of our acquisitive efforts and is preeminent as the cause of our wrongdoing.

Accepting the role of greed in our wrongdoing it follows to ask what is it that people are seeking, what is the role or object of greed?

What is it that people want? It is useful to look at greed in terms of its objective or goal. Three categories or ways of classifying acts of greed are offered. First, and perhaps most common, is our desire for earthly goods, followed by hedonism, and security.

Earthly desires encompass our persistent and continuous pursuit of more money and the things money makes possible. Persons who make money their primary goal in life never have enough. Why do they want more? There is always the haunting possibility that someone somewhere has more. Too, there is always the possibility of the rainy day, of market failures, or, forbid, outliving one's money. Power, the ability to control others and situations, is, unfortunately, an ever-present accompaniment of money. An irreverent rephrasing of the Golden Rule reads: those who have the gold make the rules. Money and power make possible all the materialistic goods that erroneously spell success. Available evidence continues to deny the idea that wealth leads to happiness.

Hedonism is the doctrine or belief that the purpose of life is to experience a maximum of physical and sensory pleasures. Titles, recognitions, pleasure, entertainment, and conspicuous consumption are evidence of having arrived. Pleasure is maximized; pain or deprivation is minimized. Such a standard of living once achieved, however, must be maintained. Unrelenting efforts are required; there can be no letting up without being branded a has-been.

Security can be defined as freedom from want or deprivation. More, bigger, and better thoughts dominate our thinking and behavior. Maintenance of our life style is goal number one. The fear of losing causes us to look at others as competitors. Interpersonal relationships become adversarial. Loss of authentic relationships is the price we pay for always wanting to win.

Greed is never good, even when defended as the means of giving to others. Such thinking was the fallacy of the movement referred to as looking out for number one. John Wesley admonished us to "earn all we can, save all we can, and give all we can," Saving and giving are made possible by earning money in socially and spiritually legitimate ways. Any defence of greediness is a wolf in sheep's clothing. It is capable of hardening our hearts and blinding our eyes to the needs of others. Economically speaking, society faces the dilemma of unlimited wants in face of limited resources. Greedy persons seek a disproportionate share of the limited resources, leaving less for others.

Greed is antithetical to Christian interpersonal relationships. "We became slaves

to many wicked desires and evil pleasures."
(Titus 3:3). Greed is detrimental to our
health and happiness. "For the world offers
only the lust for physical pleasure, the
lust for everything we are, the pride in our
possessions." (1 Jn 20:33-34).

The most serious problem facing our country
is greed—reckless and unashamed greed.
It is the excuse of the embarrassing and
disgusting financial scandals that fill our
media daily (circa 2011). Greed is the cause
of the obscene salaries and bonuses paid to
top-level corporate executives even as their
companies are failing.

30

HAPPINESS

*"When others are happy, be happy
with them. When others are sad, share
their sorrow."* Rom 12-15 (NLT)

The flow of human happiness has not always
been as smooth as the sweetness of its
name would suggest. Numerous detours and
potholes have hindered its path. Two of these
hindrances, often supported by self-serving
Biblical interpretations and consequent
social mores, have combined to keep those
who would be happy in a state of theological
and psychological bondage.

The first, an ill-conceived theological
notion, has historically questioned our right
to be happy as long as we are in a state
of sin. Happiness and sin, it is argued,
are incompatible. If we sin, we are not
entitled to happiness. If we accept the logic
(truthfulness) of this argument, we are faced
with a seemingly iron-clad dilemma. We can

not stop sinning, *ipso facto;*, we can never know happiness. An unfortunate twist of this argument causes many people to actually fear or avoid happiness, believing that if they are too happy they are going to be punished. For these people it is a sin to be happy.

Those who argue this way put undue emphasis on our sinning coupled with too little faith in God's desire and readiness to forgive our sins. God's love and grace free us from the dilemma and confirm our right to be happy. God wants us to be happy; God wants us to enjoy the spiritual, psychological, and physiological benefits of happiness. Archibald Rutledge would agree. He said, "I am absolutely unshaken in my faith that God created us, loves us, and wants us to not only to be good, but to be happy."

The second hinderance is psychological in nature and transcends the first hindrance by questioning the source of human happiness. Is happiness dependent on external circumstances or is it a matter of will? Is happiness the pot of gold at the end of the rainbow or is it the path we follow to get there? It is the journey that counts—not the destination. Happiness comes more from making progress toward goals than actually achieving them. We do not have to surrender control of our emotions (happiness is one) to forces outside ourselves.

Happiness is a human emotion; it is a state of overall well—being. Happiness does not mean an absence of problems. Everybody has problems, including happy people. But happy people have confidence in their ability to resolve their problems. In fact, being able to solve personal/interpersonal problems builds confidence and further enhances feelings of well-being. Anxiety, stress, and defeatism—characteristics of unhappy people—are pushed aside. Happy people are optimistic; their glass is always half full. Happiness is not a luxury; it is a necessity for our overall well-being.

Abraham Lincoln is often quoted as having said, "Most people are about as happy as they make up their mind to be." His remark embraces my feelings about happiness. I would, however, add a word of warning. Happiness is not a constant, uninterrupted state of well-being. It must be maintained. Happiness, like a good marriage, requires constant attention. When some Pharisees asked Jesus when the Kingdom of God would come he replied: " . . . the Kingdom of God is within you." (Lk 17:20-21).

In a like manner the question, "Where/How can I find happiness?" can best be answered by replying that we are our own source of happiness. We are the wellspring of our own happiness. No one can give it to us or take it from us without our permission. Happiness is not a result of the symbols of success. The search for externals to make us happy does not work because we are trying to forget a remembered pain. The harder we try to be happy by creating favorable external circumstances in our lives, the less likely we are to achieve it. Happiness comes from living a life that has meaning and purpose. Happiness is a by-product, never a primary goal.

A personal story illustrates the error of depending on external circumstances to make us happy. While I was practicing psychotherapy, a prominent business executive called for a late-hour appointment. The building was nearly empty when he knocked on my door. I opened the door expecting him to greet me with his hand extended. He was, instead, concentrating on something down the hall. I stepped forward so I could see what he was watching. I saw a custodial person mopping the floor. He was singing joyously and moving about as though he were dancing. Turning to me my visitor said, "If I could be that happy, I would take that mop from him and clean this floor myself."

What kind of feelings are you having about my visitor's complaint? What would you like to say to him?

31

HATE

"You have heard it was said, "Love your friends, hate your enemies.' But now I tell you: Love your enemies, and pray for those who persecute you . . . ." Mt 5:43-44 (GNB)

Former President George H. W. Bush removed all doubt when he declared "I totally hate broccoli." While many children might agree with him, it made no difference at all to broccoli. Like all instances of hate, it is the hater who suffers. In this instance the President was denying himself the good taste and nutrition of broccoli. What he possibly meant was, "I don't like broccoli, however it is prepared." His word choice was for emphasis, no doubt.

Hate can be described as a deep, enduring, intense emotion expressing animosity, anger, and even hostility toward another person, group, or object, There are no boundaries to hate; it can be found in all arenas of human activity, and the objects of our hate range from random objects (e.g., broccoli) to hatred of other people, even entire groups of people. Hate can so intense that it can and often does lead to violence. No one is immune from hatred; we are all vulnerable.

What is hate? It can be viewed from several disparate stances reflecting differing degrees of variation, depending upon the persuasions of the author. Within the diversity of definitions, however, there is still found a common core. Philosophers view hate or hatred in terms of an awareness that it is bad, combined with an urge or desire to withdraw from it. Contemporary psychology takes the view that hatred is more of an attitude or disposition than a temporary emotional state. Neurologists point to a dysfunctional pattern of brain activity that occurs when persons undergoing Magnetic Resonance Imaging (MRI) view photos of persons they hate.

Without defining hate, the Bible commands us to hate what is bad and love what is good. Biblical prohibitions against hate are found from Genesis to Revelations. In the Old Testament, a majority of references to hate are found in the so-called wisdom literature: Psalms, Proverbs, and Ecclesiastes. In the New Testament, Jesus often used the word. "You have heard it was said, 'Love your friends and hate your enemies.' But now I tell you . . . ." (Mt 15:43-44). "Whoever hates me hates my Father also." (Mt 15:23). The message of the New Testament gospels is that we must love what is good and hate what is bad. Good and bad, right and wrong are not matters for subjective interpretation and choice. They are, rather, matters for prayer and spiritual discernment. God hates lies and stealing but He loves both liars and thieves too much to leave them that way.

Psychologists are in general agreement that all human behavior is motivated behavior, i.e., the purpose of all behavior, both conscious and unconscious, is to satisfy some particular human need. Accepting the validity of this opinion, it seems appropriate to ask "Why do we hate? What need does it serve? Before seeking an answer to this question let us look at another psychological assertion: emotions such as hate do not exist in isolation—they are not independent of each other. Hate, for example, can find common ground with other emotions such as fear, anxiety, and, yes, love. Let us also ask "Why do we love?"

At some level of meaning or understanding it seems probable that we both hate and love for the same reasons. We love because we want to be connected to others, to be accepted and approved. We want to be secure. We hate others because they pose threats to our security. We feel threatened by them; they differ from us and we view them as threats to our well being. Envy and jealousy can and often do underpin and exaggerate our feelings of hate.

The conflict between loving love and hating hate and behaving accordingly is a key problem in our modern, highly-competitive society. Although we pay lip service to the ideals of "brotherly love" and seek God's guidance in avoiding hate, a mixture of hate and love complicates many of our social relationships. What can we do with the hate feelings we recognize in ourselves but see no socially approved way of expressing?

As with other emotions competence in dealing with hate feelings begins with an understanding and acceptance of our hate feelings. Changing how we feel can only begin after we accept our feelings. This does not mean we should defend and nourish our hate feelings. But to do nothing complicates our physical, psychological, and spiritual well-being. Why do I feel hatred toward others? Do I feel justified feeling as I do? How often do I have these feelings? What have others done to me? Do I hate particular people or do I hate everyone? How do I typically express my feelings of hate? What are the consequences for others and for myself? Are my hate feelings more a problem for me than for the others?

Dr. Martin Luther King was a target of intense hatred for many years, yet he was able to write, "Hatred paralyzes life; love releases it. Hatred confuses life; love harmonizes it. Hatred darken life; love illuminates it." (*Strength to Love* 1963.) With God's help, Dr. King overcame the temptation to hate those who hated him. He was able to forgive those who hated and persecuted him.

32

BEING AND DOING

"What good will it be for a man if he gains the whole world yet forfeits his soul?" Mt 16-26. (NIV)

"So you see it isn't enough just to have faith. Faith that doesn't show itself by good deeds is no faith at all—it is dead and useless." James 2:17. (NLT)

Let us begin by pretending that we can magically create or bring into being two new churches. (Warning: asking how we can do this will end the fantasy.)

In the process of creating these two new churches let us make them as much alike as we can—identical if we can. Let us begin with two congregations of equal size whose members are matched in age, gender, education, and economic and social factors. Both churches are furnished and have comparable physical facilities and equipment and supplies to do their work. They are staffed with the same number of ordained clergy and other professional staff with similar education and work experiences. Finally, let us locate these two churches in parishes that are comparable in terms of relevant demographic characteristics.

Now that we have created these two new, identical churches let us press the GO button and start them off at the same moment of time with a common understanding of a common ministry: to make disciples of Jesus Christ.

Now, let us withdraw and watch what happens as our fantasy unfolds. As we continue to observe the two churches, we notice that one of the churches is moving out in front of the other. By all relevant measures, it is more successful, more effective, more involved, more responsive. Slowly but surely, the differences between the two churches gets greater, more noticeable.

In the more successful church, the congregation comes together as a loving, caring family of believers in Christ. The members are prayerfully and actively involved in the ministries of the church, both within and in its outreach ministries. Stewardship is taken seriously; volunterism is dependable. They are loyal to their church and uphold it by their prayers, their presence, their gifts, their service, and their witness.

And now some reality. This kind of differential performance does not happen only in our fantasy, it also happens in real life. The most important question—the only question, in fact—that we should ask is, "Why?"

Churches are voluntary organizations, created to serve the spiritual needs of its members. In order to exist and achieve its stated purpose a church must attract and retain committed members. There are two separate but interrelated decisions every would-be member must make. First is the question of whether to join. Persons will join if the perceived benefits are great enough. Making the second decision—moving from just being a member to being a doing member—is more complex. Two factors complicate the process.

First, new (and older) members are often seduced by the 80/20 rule. In practice, twenty percent of the members (doers) perform eighty percent of the ministries of the church. The eighty percent (hearers only) is lulled into believing that all is well—that all the programmed ministries are being performed, and that their involvement is not needed. The second hinderance is allied to the first. While church tradition and culture tell us that doers are respected and honored, it also teaches us not to be pushy, not to assert ourselves, but to be humble in all that we do. Persons holding this view want to be called, to be coaxed; they want to feel they are being called to fill a special niche in the church.

A cartoon on my church bulletin board captured the essence of this decision dilemma. A sign at the main entrance to the sanctuary directed "Hearers" to one side and "Doers" to the other. Try to imagine the anguish of worshippers as they step through the sanctuary door. Most likely, the "Hearer" side is empty. Who would knowingly accept that label? But what does sitting on the "Doers" side mean? Is it chosen to avoid the embarrassment of being seen as a "Hearer" only, or is it a genuine commitment to be a "Doer?'

God wants all his churches to be like the more effective church in our fantasy. Obviously achieving that success would require more than twenty per cent of the members to be in meaningful ministry—a church cannot be something that its members are not. The *"why does it happen question"* must become a *"how do you do it"* question.

Paul's preachment that the righteous are justified by faith (Romans 4:5) is often used to forge a yes answer to the question, "Can one have faith without good works?" Paul was countering those who falsely believe they could earn God's favor by performing

138

good works. James (2:24) also challenged the assumption that one can have faith without works, that one can live a Christian life without obedience and sacrifice.

Who in your church will feed the hungry? Who will give a drink to the thirsty? Who will care for the sick? Who will visit the prisoner? Who will make disciples of Jesus Christ?

Hearing the Word is of limited use unless it is believed. Believing the Word will do some good if believed only, but believing the Word will do great good if it is accompanied by good works.

33

HELPING

". . . . warn the idle, encourage the timid, help the weak, be patient with everyone. See that no one pays back wrong for wrong, but at all times make it your aim to do good to one another and to all people." 1 Thes 5:14-15. (GNB)

After the verb "to love,"
"to help" is most beautiful.
This sentence is inscribed on a framed card that hangs on the wall in my office. Although the author is unknown to me, I have always thought of these words as though they were my own.

I am a licensed psychotherapist, a member of what is today being called a helping profession. Clients come to me complaining of pain, trouble, and difficulty. They want to be liberated from their problems. They come seeking help in the form of understanding, approval, acceptance, and love. There is an idea of long standing that the help I give is determined by what I do and say. This belief has given credence to learning techniques and methods in preparation for licensure and practice. But research and our own experience are today suggesting that techniques are far less important than the attitudes shown by the helper. Attitudes and the feelings they produce determine the effectiveness of the relationship between the helper and the person being helped.

That is why the framed bit of wisdom is so important to me. For my helping efforts to be effective, they must be an outgrowth of my attitude of love for all persons, a love expressed in terms of respect for their dignity and integrity. Helping, for me, is a synonym for loving.

It is a pretty safe bet that hardly a day passes without our giving or receiving help in some way. Unfortunately, we use the term "helping" to include situations where our behavior is more assistance than helping. My wife initially typed this page. Was she helping me, or merely assisting in the preparation of my book?

By helping, I refer to the things we do to make another person experience a heightened sense of worth and belief in their abilities to cope with their circumstances. An outcome of helping, in my view, is causing a change from feeling discouraged to feeling encouraged, from harboring feelings of revenge to showing forgiveness. It is not enough that we want to promote the psychological and spiritual well-being of others—we must seek these outcomes for their sake, not our own. Helping is always other-person centered. Helping behavior is also distinguished by both its motives and its consequences. That is why it so important to know ourselves. Without this self knowledge it is unlikely we can achieve desired outcomes.

Implied in the preceding paragraph are two important ideas. First, we can behave in a helping role only when we intend to help. Without this goal or purpose, our behavior becomes random; it may or may not be helpful. Secondly, we can translate our intentions into effective helping behavior only when we possess the prerequisite social and attitudinal skills. The major problem we face in helping others is acting in ways that are consistent with our attitudes and feelings of love.

Helping is using our gifts and graces to minister to others. Helping is responding to the needs of others. Helping is being a good Samaritan, righting wrongs, and visiting hospitals and jails. Helping is seeing a problem and solving it, or a conflict and resolving it. Helping is bringing others into fellowship with Christ.

We have the mind of Christ in us when we have an active concern for the well-being of everyone. Concern means we want some valued end for them. Our concern for them means that it matters to us. Wishful thinking or just passively longing for that end is not enough. Our concern must be active; we must behave in ways intended to bring about that end.

We can best show our love and concern for others by relating to them in an adult-to-adult relationship. When we unknowingly slip into a parent-to-child role, the message we send out is "I'm O. K., you're not O. K." This message inevitably causes the other person to lose trust and become suspicious and defensive.

Acts of helping behavior do not have to be consciously planned. Everything we do, consciously or unconsciously, has an effect upon others. Is this effect helpful or hurting? What effect do we intend? We should always behave toward others in ways that will build them up, that will promote their psychological and spiritual well-being.

Try to imagine the cumulative effect if all members of God's family here on earth showed an active concern for the well-being of others. Wow! That is exactly what God wants us to do.

34

HOLINESS

"God did not call us to live in immorality, but in holiness."
1 Thes 4:7. (GNB)

Holiness is a genuine, exclusive Biblical word; it is unique in that there is no equivalent secular word. It has a mystique, a sense of diviness, majesty, and glory. It is both comforting and challenging. Understandably, it is often misunderstood. Yet, it cannot be ignored or dismissed; nor can it be taken for granted. Why? God requires it. "But now you must be holy in everything you do, just as God—Who chose you to be His children—is holy. For He Himself has said, 'You must be holy because I am holy'." (1 Pet 1:15-16) The command to be holy implies the practicability of becoming so. Yet, the most sincere, willing response to God's call to be holy leads us to some well-intentioned questions. What is holiness? What does it mean to be holy? How do we become holy?

Before answering the above questions let us try to grasp the essence of God's holiness.

Anyone beginning a study of the Bible is quickly confronted with the word holy. Judging from its frequent and wide usage—from Exodus to Revelation—holy is elevated to a distinctly divine usage in helping us to formulate a conception of God. The word finds its fulfillment in referring to God alone, as though God co-opted the word for His own. It is the word God used to reveal Himself to us. Holiness is the very essence of God's being; it is not merely an attribute of God—God is the attribute of holiness. God is holy in his nature and all His works of creation attest to His holiness. His love is holy. His mercy is holy, His judgments are holy, even His wrath and anger are holy. He is the source and cause of all that is holiness in others. What is God like? Jesus provided an all encompassing answer when He spoke plainly to the doubting Jews, "I and the Father (God) are one." (Jn 10:30) And later, responding to Philip, Jesus said, "Anyone who has seen me has seen the Father." (Jn 14:9)

Now, what does it mean for us to be holy? A short answer is to be Christ like. While we would glory in that answer we would no doubt want some guidance so as not to miss the mark. The Hebrew word most often translated as "holy" in the Bible has the literal meaning of "set apart, separate." Applied to believers, this translation implies we are called by God to be distinct, set aside for God's purposes, living our daily lives according to His instructions and standards. Accepting and trying earnestly to live by God's rules in our daily lives automatically sets us apart—that we have rejected the rules of the world and chosen to be part of God's earthly family.

As we respond to God's command to be holy, we dependably fall into the trap of believing that we have to be free of sin. This we can not do, but we can, as Paul writes, not be a slave to sin, having chosen to be a slave to Jesus Christ. (Rom 6:6) Hating sin in our lives, we turn to a merciful God and find Him always ready to forgive us. His grace paves the way for us to experience His holiness as we live for Him in obedience to His plan for our lives.

The cornerstone of living a life filled with God's holiness has four unmistakable dimensions. First is the idea that we belong to God. We are His creations; He has called us His own; He is the creator, giver, and preserver of our lives. We are uniquely His. Second, and to be emphasized, is that we are members of God's earthly family, We live with

Him as Head of His family, as a loving and caring Father. He wants us to live with and for Him, to know and share His holiness.

A third dimension of the cornerstone is the fact that as we grow and mature in God's holiness we take on a holistic (wholeness) identity. Christ's teachings in His Sermon on the Mount (The Beatitudes) and the fruits of the Spirit all combine into a fabric of righteous living.

The fourth dimension is our submission to a dependent relationship with God. It is a relationship filled with praise and thanksgiving for God's fatherly love and concern for us—for the privilege of being chosen as His adopted children.

As believers, we have been blessed with God's gift of an open-door relationship. What does God ask of us? That we live a set-apart life, living according to His word as it is revealed to us.

35

HONESTY

"No more lying, then! Each of you must tell the truth to the other believer, because we are all members together in the body of Christ."
Eph. 4:25. (GNB)

Imagine that as you start your morning drive to work, you notice that the fuel gauge is on the three-quarter mark. After a few miles on the expressway, the engine sputters and stops—you are out of gas. Your gas gauge lied to you. You depended on the gas gauge for a truthful measurement and it lied to you. It is the same way when people lie. Lying is fatal to our sense of psychological and spiritual well-being, and our physical and material security.

Lying is the most pervasive of all sins; all of us have lied, and all of us have been lied to. Lying has so many faces, serves so many purposes, and assumes so many shades of gray that categorizing them would be a seemingly impossible task. In spite of the dilemmas and complexities created by changing societal norms about lying, there is one common denominator to them all. Whatever their relationship to the truth, we lie to deceive. However we distort the truth in lying, our goal is always to cause others to believe something we know to be false.

The Cadets at the United States Air Force Academy live under an honor code which provides; "We will not lie, steal, or cheat nor will we tolerate among us those who do." The faculty and staff who interact with the cadets are also expected to live by the provisions of the code—to be role models and provide a supportive environment. During the seven years I taught at the Academy I experienced a microcosm of the kind of earthly society God wants for us. Honesty and respect were the hallmarks of everyone's thoughts and behavior. My office had no door; my desk had no lock. Examinations were never proctorred. Cameras, calculators, wallets, etc., left in classrooms remained there until recovered by the owners. Yes, there were occasional violations of different kinds and degrees; but there was never a cadet who left the Academy without feelings of sorrow and loss by everyone, including the transgressor. It was not too unlike violations of God's rule against lying, with the exception that God forgives.

The results of a 1994 survey of Americans' manners and morals show how far we have deviated from the society of the Air Force Academy, In the survey, the results of which were published with the title, *The Day America Told the Truth,* the respondents were constantly reminded of the need to be truthful. And a good thing they were. In the spirit of telling the truth, ninety-one percent of the respondents admitted to lying at times. Ironically, an almost equal number stated they believed in God. "How can that be?" we ask. How can people believe in God and at the same time disobey His commandments? What is the answer to this paradox of believing and lying?

Is it because lying is such a complicated subject, because it is so widely practiced, or because it no longer serves any useful purpose to distinguish between those who lie and those who do not? Has lying gained a mark of respectability and acceptability because everyone does it? Has lying become a socially approved behavior for adjusting to uncertain, changing values and circumstances? Is it OK to lie in order to avoid criticism, embarrassment, or ridicule? Do liars no longer care if others know?

Entertaining these questions leads us into a blind alley. Let us look at the truth about lying. All lies are told with the intent to mislead. Whether our lies conceal or falsify, whether we tell them to gain advantage or hide our cowardice, we lie to manipulate the responses of others. We seek an advantage that we would not otherwise have. Lying leaves us in a conflicted, win-lose relationship with others. If there were no benefit to be gained from lying, why bother?

Despite the process of changing times and shifting values, honesty remains an indispensable, prized virtue. God recognized that His earthly family could co-exist only upon a bedrock of interpersonal honesty. He wants us to live in harmonious relationships with others. Our happiness, our sense of spiritual and psychological well-being, and our relationships with others all depend upon honesty. Without honesty, there is no basis for relationships.

In a perfect society—the kind God wants for us—there would be neither motive nor context for telling lies. Truth, openness, and integrity would be upheld; deception would be detested. All lies are sins because they violate the nature of God; lies separate us from God and from His family.

36

HOPE

"When the true message, the Good News, first came to you, you heard about the hope it offers. So your faith and love are based on what you hope for, which is kept safe for you in heaven." Col 1:5. (GNB)

An experiment reported in many psychology texts helps us to understand what hope is. Several rats were placed in a container of water, with sides too tall for climbing and water too deep for standing. All the rats could do was swim. After a few minutes, the rats would stop swimming and drown. One rat was removed from the water after it stopped swimming but before it actually drowned. Later the same rat was again placed in the container of water and was able to swim for more than 24 hours. The rats that drowned after a few minutes could have swam for much longer; they simply gave up because they had no hope. The long-endurance rat had hope, based upon its previous experience that someone would rescue it. It had hope but no faith.

Ask someone to construct a sentence using the word hope. and chances are that it will be used as a verb. "I hope I can get a job after I graduate." "I hope it will not rain this weekend." Or, in a more serious vein, "I hope they soon find a cure for cancer." Without any past experience that would control or predict the future, there is no promise of a positive outcome, however strong and sincere our hopes may be. Wishful thinking can be positive in some small ways, but there are no real grounds for waiting for desired outcomes. Still, I am sure that the long-endurance rat was wishing that its rescuer would soon come. Hope kept the rat swimming even as it was losing its strength.

Hope is equally powerful, whether of secular or spiritual persuasion. By this I mean that secular hope can motivate a person to action just as powerfully as Biblical hope that comes from the promises of God. The important difference is that Biblical hope is based on the acts of God in the past. His past actions give substance to His promises of the future. God's promises have been vindicated through the death and resurrection of Jesus the Messiah. There is really no hope where uss Holloman, Ph.D.

there are no promises and there is no faith without hope.

Hope is futuristic. Our hope for the future is based upon what God has done in the past. We embrace hope as a theological virtue because its immediate object is God (1 Cor.13:13). This hope about the future buttresses our faith; it strengthens and motivates us to keep going in the present. Hope works on the human heart and motivates us to remain steadfast in our faith, even in the face of doubt. Hebrews 11:1 says that faith is the substance of things hoped for. I take this to mean that faith is being convinced about the things we hope for. Hope and faith encompass our response to the eternal plan of God for those who believe in Jesus.

Our understanding of hope is made more pragmatic by considering what the state of hopelessness is like. The rats that drowned after two minutes of swimming saw no purpose in continuing. Hopelessness is loneliness; it is isolation, and easily leads to despair and depression. Without hope the human spirit spirals downward to destruction. During my years of practicing psychotherapy I lost one patient by suicide. Although the circumstances of his life were tragically unfavorable, his medications helped him to maintain a semblance of well being. "Do I have to take these pills the rest of my life?" he asked.

In desperation, without hope, he provided his own answer to his question. Many people place their hope in such unpromising things as knowledge or technology. Such hope is in vain. Only those who's hope is in God can claim it with certainty. Hope for Christians has to do with the things God has promised—things that we have not yet seen. Our faith dictates that what God has promised God can and will deliver. Our hope is fortified by our faith, and it gives our faith the vital quality of endurance.

37

HUMILITY

. . . *"Whoever wants to be first must place himself last of all and be the servant of all."* Mk 9:35b. (GNB)

High school and college commencement speakers dependably urge graduates to be ambitious, to set high goals, and become all that they can be. These speakers suggest that societal and economic rewards come to those who prepare and work for them. A lifestyle of affluence, recognition, and status is the goal. To choose anything other is a forfeiture of opportunities and a rejection of the gospel of success.

Why would anyone reject the gospel of success when society admires and envies the lifestyle the of rich and famous? Would not everyone choose to be prominent with stories and photos of accomplishments in the local papers, and a resume entitling them to sit at the head table? Is not this what everyone would choose: to be seen as successful individuals who have in place all the pieces of the success puzzle? In a society holding these values, humility has little to recommend it. Anything that goes against the acquisitive grain of human nature is summarily rejected.

For much of our social history, the word humility has been used in a judgmental, derogatory manner. It was/is widely regarded as a sign of weakness and failure in the game of life. Humble persons are characteristically perceived as having missed the boat of success. Because of the stigma attached to it, humility remains in low estate.

Being humble does not mean an absence of abilities and achievements, nor does worldly success negate humility. Humility and world success are not incompatible. A message on a marque at an auto repair shop (itself a humble place) captured the essence of this point: it read, "Humility is feeling embarrassed when others praise you." I couldn't think of anything I could add to this statement. I wanted to share it with you because it contains two essential truths. First, humble people can produce praiseworthy outcomes in their work. Second, humility is most genuine when it outlives the praiseworthy event. The latter truth easily reminds us that there is no limit as to what we can do if we don't care who gets the credit.

Jesus affirmed that He was the Son of God, giving Him the highest possible stature. Yet, throughout His ministry He showed humility by giving credit to God for all the wondrous deeds He performed and the praises He received. He demonstrated humility; He taught humility. He found His humility by seeing Himself in relation to God. Likewise, if we want humility it can only come by comparing ourselves to Jesus. To say that we are more humble than our neighbor is meaningless. The standard of humility is God, not our neighbor. John the Baptist understood this when He said, "He (Jesus) must increase, but I must decrease" John 3:30. Micah, too, recognized the importance of humility by declaring it a virtue to characterize anyone who claims to know God (Micah 6:8).

Jesus began His Sermon on the Mount by blessing the low in spirit (the humble). He made humility a precondition for knowing and receiving the blessings to follow. Can we mourn believing that our own strength is sufficient for all the problems of life? No. Can we hunger and thirst for righteousness if we boast about our own righteousness? No. Can we be merciful without recognizing our own need for mercy? No. Can we seek purity of our heart if it is filled with pride? No. Can we be a peacemaker if we feel we are always right? No.

Why press the point further? Humility is not an option; it is a necessity—a precondition for living a Christian life. Either we walk humbly with God or we do not walk with God at all.

38

JOY

"When you obey me, you remain in my love, just as I obey my Father and remain in His love. I have told you this so that you will be filled with my joy. Yes, your joy will overflow."
Jn 15:10-11 (NLT)

A member of the Sunday School class I teach attended a weekend Emmaus Walk. The following Sunday, he was asked to share the experience for us. He described four or five peak events or activities, seemingly unable to paint a holistic picture of the weekend for us. Finally, in a fit of resignation he declared, "I'm sorry for not being more helpful. It's hard to put into words. You'll have to find out for yourself."

His plight reminded me of a prologue to a movie I saw years ago, a Hemingway story, I believe. A rewording of the prologue seemed appropriate. "For those who have attended an

Emmaus Walk, no explanation is necessary; for those who haven't no explanation is adequate." Another member of the class, also trying to be helpful, shared that he had read somewhere of a famous jurist who said, "I can't define pornography but I know it when I see it."

These scenarios remind us that we find it difficult to give a precise, universally acceptable definition of joy. But we, too, know it when we experience it. We remember the occasions of joy because they stand apart from lesser experiences of contentment and well being; they nourish us; they help us to look at situations with a different set of eyes. We want joy to stay.

Joy is a human emotion all people can experience whatever their circumstances in life. The fact that joy is hard to define has unfortunately clothed it as a mystique. Joy does not have to be defined to be experienced, nor does joy come to all persons in the same ways under similar circumstances. Joy is not a one-size fits all experience. Joy calls some individuals to dance, others to sing, and others to rest with contentment.

Previously I wrote about happiness (30. HAPPINESS}. I wanted to discuss the emotion of happiness apart from the emotion of joy. It was not my purpose, however, to present happiness as being unrelated to joy, as is widely argued. In a sense, happiness and

joy are "kissing cousins" or opposite sides
of the same coin. Can we know joy without
being happy about it. Can we be happy without
knowing some of the feeling of joy? Why can't
we be happy and joyful at the same time?
Where does happiness end and joy begin?
The dictionary definitions of happiness and
joy are remarkably similar. Still, we take
comfort in thinking of happiness as a secular
psychological experience and of joy as a
divine or heavenly experience. Joy does have
the connotation of being a grander, more
enduring state of mind. Some words associated
with joy include delight, praise, faith, and
service. But joy is also associated with
adversity, sacrifice, and suffering. All of
these associations, both positive and negative,
give joy its fullness and elevating quality.

My Bible concordance contains numerous
references to the nouns joy and joyfulness,
and to the verb rejoice. The sheer number
of these references suggest that "rejoice"
might be the most frequent command in the
Bible. Apart from the Bible and Christmas
cards, however, the word joy has little usage
suggesting that joy is primarily a distinctive
Biblical word and that joyfulness is a unique
Christian experience. One might conclude that
God has co-opted the word, using it for His
own purposes. God of the Bible is a joyful
God and He wants to share His joy—so we can

have both the attitude and personality of joy. Our prayers for joy are always answered "Yes!"

"Try me," God might say, "I'll share my own joy with you."

39

JUDGING

"Do not judge, or you too will be judged. For in the same way you judge others, you too will be judged, and with the same measure you use, it will be measured to you." Mat 7:1-2. (NIV)

Yesterday, 20 July 2010, was primary election day in Georgia.

I entered the voting booth with my crib sheet in hand, feeling good about my choices. Some of the incumbents had no opposition. I could either vote for or withhold my vote for them. It was a decision—a judgement—I had to make. In the contested races, I had to decide which candidate I would vote for. How does one decide these matters? I listened to their speeches; I read their campaign literature; and I tried to objectively evaluate what their opponents were saying about them. And after wading through the mudslinging, I made my choices. To vote is to make a judgment for or against a particular candidate. Voting always confronts me with reservations and the dangers of making subjective judgments about ill-defined personal characteristics.

Jesus wisely anticipated the temptations and pitfalls of our making judgments about others. His preachment against judging others is arguably the most quoted Bible verse, with the possible exception of John 3-16. As we glibly quote Matthew 7:1, we would do ourselves and others well to pray for a full understanding of what Jesus meant in the context of His other preachments about judging. He had a lot more to say about judging than the one sentence. After condemning unrighteous, hypocritical judging on the one hand, a few verses later He warned us against evildoers and false prophets and those who practice all kinds of evil. How can we avoid the evildoers without making judgments about them? When Jesus condemned judging, He was not in any manner implying that we should never make judgments about others. He was warning us against heaping criticism and condemnation upon others before looking critically at our behavior. Simply put, we are forbidden to judge hypocritically.

As I write my understanding of what Jesus meant I realize that, in a sense, I am judging. (Shouldn't I say guilty of judging?) With my understanding, however, I feel outside Jesus' condemnation of wrongful judging. What Jesus condemned was a self-serving, hypocritical spirit, a sense of spiritual superiority. Jesus was particularly critical of our practice of judging the speck in the eye of others while blinded by the log in our own eye. He commanded us to first examine ourselves for the problems we are quick to judge in others. In today's language, Jesus was telling us to get our own house in order before we judge others. Even then, the question of motivation is critical. Do we sincerely seek to help others; are we capable of showing love, understanding, and forgiveness? Do we have a righteous spirit? Do we have the spirit of Jesus?

Judging others is most vicious and morally wrong when it reflects a sense of superiority on our part. This implies an assumption that we can build ourselves up by putting others down. Equally objectionable is the idea that we can justify ourselves by projecting onto others characteristics we do not like about ourselves. Psychologists define this practice as projection; it is viewed as a defense mechanism. Jesus would call it hypocrisy, a human weakness that He is especially critical of.

In our modern societal culture, with its emphasis on diversity, tolerance, and political correctness, there is a tendency to not judge for what at first glance seems to be complying with Jesus' preachment. In truth, we choose not to judge others or situations for fear that we will be accused of being judgmental. According to this argument, ironically, when we are accused of being judgmental, the accuser is being judgmental—another example of hypocrisy.

Clearly, not all judging is forbidden. As Christians we are expected to judge and speak against those things that Jesus' condemned, e.g., sexual permissiveness, social injustice, and hunger. If we, as Christians, do not make these righteous judgments, who will?

40

KINDNESS

"You are the people of God; He loved you and chose you for His own. So then, you must clothe yourselves with compassion, kindness, gentleness, and patience." Col 3:12. (GNB)

While basking in the warm sun, a scorpion asked a nearby frog to give him a ride across the lake. The frog refused, explaining that he had heard frightening stories about the scorpion's bites. But the scorpion countered, "It would be crazy for me to bite you as we crossed the lake, why, both of us would drown." The argument persuaded the frog and he invited the scorpion to get on his back. As the frog paddled across the lake, he felt the sting of the scorpion's bite and angrily demanded, "Why did you do that?" "That's just the say I am." replied the scorpion.

Kindness is a moral virtue, and every Christian should be able to defend their predisposition to kindness with "That's just the way I am." The adjective kind can be used to describe a person or action of that person. Unless the person is predisposed to kindness through social and church upbringing his action could be for selfish reasons. Consider the following scenario described by Scott Peck (*A World Waiting to be Born*):

Flying at 30 thousand feet over Nebraska, a business executive saw his seat mate as a possible business prospect. He considered buying the person a drink, but first excused himself and used the plane phone to check the person's Dunn and Bradstreet rating. He returned to his seat and bought a beer for his new best friend.

What is wrong with this story? Why does it bother us? Buying his new friend a beer could easily be seen as a kind gesture, but we see his behavior as self serving, which violates the essence of kindness. Kindness is shown to others in order to improve their circumstances. We show kindness because we want to improve the circumstance of the other person(s). We might be viewed more favorably when we are perceived as being kind, but that must never be our motivation.

Why do some people view acts of kindness with suspicion while others see the same acts as adding to the store house of goodness in the world? Why do some people equate kindness with weakness while others counter that only strong people can be kind? Why do some people refrain from even simple acts of kindness for fear of being taken advantage of? Why do others look for goodness in all people and respond to them with kindness?

Each of these questions moves us to the fork in the road where we look at our own values and choices as to own behavior. We live by values, and they play a major role in determining our behavior. We are free to choose. The opposite of kindness is not unkindness, it is no kindness. And it is frightening to even consider living in a society where there is no kindness.

I recall a story of a family who celebrated Thankful Thursday. Each member of the family was supposed to perform an act of kindness and tell the other family members about it at dinner on Thursday. It is a beautiful story but were the acts of kindness performed in order to have something to tell at dinner, or were they performed because "That's the way I am?" This difference can also be noted in a local elementary school that awarded prizes to students who read six books during the school year. No students claimed to have read seven. Did they read six books to earn the prize, or did they read because they enjoyed reading?

I like to add the adjective loving to kindness, to hyphenate it as loving-kindness. Loving-kindness overflows into compassion as we empathize with others' difficulties. If, however, we feel pity for other persons, we are mimicking the spirit of loving-kindness without empathy. Only when we are filled with love are we ready to show loving-kindness to others.

Jesus was the epitome of kindness. Read the story of how He related to the woman at the well (Jn 4:4-26). If we, as Christians, seek to live a Christian life style, we must clothe ourselves with the kindness of Jesus. Kindness is love; it is a creative force. Kindness is a lovely word for a lovely quality. Like a smile, kindness can make a difference in our relations with others.

41

LOVE

"After breakfast, Jesus said to Simon Peter, 'Simon, son of John, do you love (agape) me more than these'?"

"Yes, Master, you know I love (philia) you." (Jn 21:15a) (Msg)

"What is this thing called love?" The perennial question asked in song by lyricist Cole Porter is one we have all pondered. We use the word a lot, poets and song writers have a field day with it. But despite its central importance in human affairs the subject of love has received surprisingly little scientific study. Too mushy, can't be quantified, and too hard to track down, are reasons given for the lack of scientific interest in the subject. Yet, most psychologists would probably agree that the ability to give and receive love is prerequisite to healthy human development and functioning.

In spite of the attending difficulties, efforts have been made to define love. Most of these efforts were initially directed toward defining the unique aspects of love feelings toward different objects of love. Drawing from the available research, four different love relationships have been delineated; three of them appear in the Bible. In the Greek language, four different words are used to describe these love relationships; in the English language we try to describe them with one word. Since our English word love is used so broadly, using the Greek words helps us to better understand the differences.

The first word, *eros*, describes romantic love. This is the love we are feeling when we declare, "I'm in love" This is the kind of love Cole Porter had in mind when he asked "What is the thing called love?" When my wife and I professed our love for the other, we were no doubt expressing feelings of eros. But we soon recognized the fickle nature of eros and our love grew gradually, but dependably, into the higher levels of love. This kind of love dependably culminates in marriage, as it did for us. The next kind, in Greek called *philia,* is what we define as brotherly love—the feelings of attraction between friends. It is from this word that we have Philadelphia, the "City of Brotherly Love." It is a dispassionate, virtuous love;

it was what Peter was feeling when he tried to assure Jesus of his love. Although both *eros* and *philia* have others as the objects of their focus, both can be motivated by self-interest and self-gratification. There is an element of giving in both, but it is for the purpose of getting something in return. The third Greek word for love is *storge*, which we use to describe motherly or parental love and caring. Today, it is used almost exclusively to describe relationships within the family.

Before discussing *agape*, the fourth word used in the Bible for love, I want to consider four additional questions surrounding love. First of these is the question of what is love, which in turn is closely related to the question of why we love. Two other matters of importance are the questions of self love, and, lastly, developing the ability to both give and receive love.

Both psychologists and theologians are willing to agree, with some reservations, that love involves empathy with/for the loved one. The lover is deeply concerned about the welfare, happiness, and well being of the loved one. Love is often defined as a feeling rather than a matter of the will. This definition supports the practice of falling out of love, particularly in the domain of eros. Why do we love? Some argue that we are hard wired for love, that it's in our DNA. A more persuasive argument is that since we are made in the image of God, and since God is Love, we are called to love like God, especially agape. One more explanation of why we love focuses on our awareness of our separateness and our need to overcome the resulting anxiety by achieving and maintaining relationships with others.

Since love for others is considered a virtue, love for the self is often assumed to be a vice. If we love ourselves, the argument goes, how can we love others? Granted, selfishness and egotistical self-love leave little room for loving others, but we cannot give to others something that we don't have. We love God—the creator—we must also love God's creations. Love for self makes possible love for others.

Many fear giving and/or receiving love because of the dependency feelings it creates. They do not like the feeling of being vulnerable—the hurt when love leaves, when lovers fall out of love. Like other emotional competencies, the ability to give and receive love depends upon such factors as self-understanding, overall level of maturity, and freedom from the need for self-defense.

The highest level of love is *Agape;* it soars above the other three and stands in contrast to them. Agape is the complete giving of yourself to others for their sake and well-being. The reason agape soars high is because it is based upon a commitment—a decision rather than a feeling alone. Agape is love because of what it does, not how it feels. Agape is an exercise of the will, a deliberate choice. God so loved (agape) that He sacrificed His Son on the cross. Surely, it did not make God feel good to do that, but it was the loving thing to do. In turn, Jesus so loved (agape) that He willingly went to the cross. He didn't want to die, but it was the loving thing to do. The Love Chapter in First Corinthians (Chapter 13) brings agape into sharp focus.

Although agape differs from the other three levels of love, it has the power to enrich others. It can create the environment where others can grow and survive. When a spouse chooses to speak and act toward the other with agape, their love escapes the bounds of external circumstances and perceptions. Parents who stay through the night by the beside of a sick child have transcended the bounds of storge and are acting at the level of agape. The person who willingly donates a kidney to an ailing neighbor transcends the bounds of philia and expresses agape to the neighbor.

As Christians, we must be obedient to all four kinds of love. We need agape because many of the things God commands of us are neither fun nor easy, but must be done. We need philia because of the joy and rewards of friendships; philia enriches our lives and gives us a sense of being accepted. It helps us to feel connected to all of God's creation. We need storge love because the affection that the human family fosters helps us to feel connected to God's spiritual family.

Using words to define love can be compared to the difficulty faced in describing the taste of ice cream. Words fail us. Both love and ice cream have to be experienced.

Jesus taught His disciples that the world would know that they were His disciples if they would show love toward one another. John 13:33.

42

MATURITY

"When I was a child, I talked like a child, I thought like A child, I reasoned like a child. When I became a man, I put childish ways behind me." 1 Corn 13:11. (NIV)

". . . . it's hard to explain because you are slow to learn. In fact, though by this time you ought to be teachers, you need someone to teach you the elementary truths of God's word all over again. You need milk, not solid food. Anyone who lives on milk, being still an infant is not acquainted with the teaching about righteousness." Heb 5:12-13 (NIV).

Spend a few minutes with your family photo album. It's embarrassing, but look at the early infant pictures of yourself.

Then follow on through early childhood, the teen years, young adulthood, and, finally, the most recent. "My, how I have changed," is a predictable response. The photos tell the story of physical change; they do not tell the story of change in other areas of your life: personality, intellectual, emotional, interpersonal competence, reasoning, and, yes, spiritual. Most of the change you're noting just happened; it was random, unplanned. Looking both back and forward, realizing that change is inevitable, you perhaps decide that it is time to intervene in the change process: to plan normative, desired changes in your life—to make happen the things you want to happen. Decisions have to be made about things you want to move away from and things you want to move toward.

Change in any area of our lives is never a static, isolated happening. Change in any one area both affects and is affected by change in other areas. The relationship is interdependent. You need a movie camera to catch the dynamic of the change process—a box camera can not do it. This is particularly true of spiritual change, because it's not something you just decide to do. It is a matter of experience, study, prayer, discipline, and savoring an ongoing relationship with God.

When words fail us in describing something we are tempted to say, "Well, I can't describe it but I know it when I see it." And it's that way with spiritual maturity. We can

bring together a long list of adjectives that
seem to fit, but no one of them captures the
big picture of a spiritually mature person.
We typically think of a spiritually mature
person as being older, believing that age and
maturity go hand in hand. But a believer can
be young in years and still evidence maturity
beyond his years. Conversely, a believer can
be a senior citizen but only a babe on the
journey to spiritual maturity. Gray hair and
longevity do not necessarily correlate with
spiritual maturity.

There is also a tendency to equate maturity
with knowledge of the Bible and the ability
to utter long spontaneous prayers.

These two factors can easily be mastered
without corresponding life changes. Solomon
accepted this truth when he cried, "Vanity,"
after discovering the folly of accumulated
human wisdom. (Ecc 2:9-15) Neither are spiritual
gifts a decisive measure or indicator of
maturity. All believers possess spiritual
gifts of some variety and measure. but mere
possession does not guarantee maturity. The
true worth of spiritual gifts is realized when
they are used to produce the fruits of the
Spirit in the lives of believers. Spiritual
gifts are a necessary but insufficient condition
of maturity.

Believers might be tempted to take a short
cut to maturity and try to follow the example

of Jesus in all areas of their lives. This is like reaching for the moon; Jesus raised the bar too high for mortals to follow in His tracks. We do grow in maturity as we become *Christlike* but we can never just imitate and exercise the qualities and capacities of Jesus; He was the only mature, perfect person. Everything about Jesus was attuned to doing the will of God.

Two questions remain about the subject of spiritual maturity. First is the question of definition. Authoritative dictionaries define it simply as a "state of full development," which leaves us with the question of what is meant by full development. Maturity is an abstract construct, it is difficult to define and even more difficult to measure or quantify.

The second question is "How does a believer attain it?" Too often, we have looked for the answer in all the wrong places. We have depended upon our own efforts, believing that it is something that we had to work to achieve. Our search for an answer must begin and end with our seeking the wisdom of the Holy Spirit. Rather than depending upon our own abilities and understandings we must surrender our will to the will of the Holy Spirit. As we journey toward spiritual maturity, we must pray for the guidance of the Holy Spirit, our helper and our counselor.

As we mature, we can confess with confidence that it is not the wisdom of the self but the Wisdom of the Holy Spirit in us. How far and how fast we progress in our journey toward maturity is never determined by our own personal abilities and wisdom, but rather by our willingness to depend upon the Lord and to allow the Spirit to guide us, as it will.

43

MORALITY

"*God did not call us to live in immorality, but in holiness.*"
1 Thes 4:7. (GNB)

"*Show yourself in all respects a model of good works, and in your teaching show integrity, gravity, and sound speech that cannot be censured; then any opponent will be put to shame, having nothing evil to say of us.*" Tit 2:7-8. (NRSV)

Can we have peaches without cream? Yes. Can a horse and a carriage have a separate existence? Again, the answer is yes. Can we separate morality from religion? The answer here is yes and no, or, more precisely, it all depends. Attempts to answer the latter question are unproductive until the terms or words being used are defined, which is seldom the case. In our contemporary understanding and usage of the word, morality is defined as a doctrine or system of moral conduct, clearly distinguishing what is right from what is wrong. But this definition by no means settles the matter, it raises still more questions which, in turn, provides fuel for even more contested argument. What do we mean by the word moral? How was the doctrine or system developed? Is it a static, closed system or is it constantly evolving? What force or authority does it have upon individual behavior?

These questions can best be answered by recognizing and defining morality at two different hierarchial levels. First, there is the matter of individual morality, which presumably is peculiar to the individual. Whether it is recognized or not, every individual has some ideas about right and wrong. Then there is the matter of a societal or unified morality, which is accepted and supported by society at large. In between there are various subgroups, e.g., outlaw groups, street gangs, and the MAFIA.

Before discussing these three levels of morality a more complete useful definition of morality is needed. Morality is the word we use to encompass systems and standards of right and wrong behavior. It is not a matter of laws although its standards are often legislated into law. Morality is concerned with how a moral person should behave.

Morality encompasses the ground rules for socially correct behavior, and is concerned with what is morally proper as opposed to what is anti-social and self-serving. In this sense, morality is the glue that holds society together.

Without a unified morality, every individual is free to choose and make up their own moral code. Fortunately, most people adopt the morality of the larger society, though they do not always abide by it. Others, unfortunately, adopt self-serving moral codes without any concern for the larger society. Individual morality, as might be expected, causes a lot of disagreement. What one person finds permissible, another finds objectionable. By definition, a personal morality is peculiar to the individual and, lacking a core value system, is subject to change as suits the whims of the holder. Any ethical code or system of morality that is always changing does not provide the guidance we need to live in harmony with others; it does not serve the purpose for which it was intended.

What is a proper basis for a moral code that is accepted and supported by society at large? Do we want a code that is absolute, that is black and white in defining what is right and wrong, or one that is filled with shades of grayness? Do we want a morality of our making or one that is grounded in a higher authority? Do we want a morality that provides everyone with ready-made excuses for anti-social behavior or a morality that makes individual behavior accountable to the larger society and, ultimately, to the source of goodness supporting our morality? There is no sense of accountability if we choose to live by a code that means whatever we say it means—that is subject to change as suits our momentary needs. If we want a code that is absolute in defining what is right and what is wrong—a morality that is the same yesterday, today, and tomorrow—there is only one source or basis. For Christians, that source is God. Only God is unchanging, giving us a morality that guides and constrains our behavior in all circumstances of life. Since God has made Himself and His righteousness known to us (Rom 1:17&19), we are without excuses in failing to live by His definition of what is right and wrong. His rules and the reasons for His rules are clear and applicable to all.

44

MURDER

"Do not commit murder."
Ex 20:13. (GNB)

Murder is high on my list of ugly words. It is not a four-letter word nor is it on the forbidden list of ten obscene words. It is not a politically incorrect word or a socially inappropriate word. It is simply an ugly word, because it violates the sacredness of human life. Human life involves the creative action of God and what is created belongs to the Creator. Since we belong to God no one, under any circumstances can claim or exercise the right to end the life of an innocent human being.

In the King James Bible the word kill is used in the Sixth Commandment instead of the word murder. There is, however, a consensus in modern translations that the original Hebrew text—the language of the Old Testament—is accurately translated to mean "You shall not murder." Murder is used to refer to the premeditated taking of an innocent human life whereas the term kill refers to unplanned, unintentional taking of a human life. All murder is killing, but not all killing is murder. This distinction usefully allows us to accept the killing of animals and plants as food sources and to focus more purposefully on the premeditated taking of innocent human life.

This distinction is useful, but it is not without difficulties. Recent advances in medical technology, accompanied by a declining influence of Christian morality, has confronted us with new life and death issues that were rare or non-existent before. Chief among these issues are abortion, euthanasia, right to die, assisted suicide, stem cell research, mercy killing, and advance medical directives. There are legal and ethical issues associated with each of these practices.

With abortion, which is now legal, there is the question of when life begins. Logically, physically, and spiritually, the evidence supports the conclusion that life begins at conception, not the day after or the hundredth day after. The killing of an unborn infant is murder, although to ease the conscience of proponents it is referred to as a fetus. Abortion in cases of rape, danger to the life of the mother, etc., present additional moral concerns.

Euthanasia is the practice of deliberately terminating the life of a person who is suffering from a painful or incurable physical sickness or accident. If it is requested by the suffering individual in an advance medical directive, it is suicide; if decided by others authorized to make life and death decisions, it is murder. (The hospital where my late wife, Lenora, died, required her to provide an advance medical directive. After several months of continuous hospitalization, she went into a coma. I was told by her attending doctors that it was my decision when to "pull the plug." After much prayer and discussions with our children, I agreed to give my decision on Tuesday morning after Labor Day 2008. Lenora died on Labor Day afternoon while still on life support systems, circumventing the presumed judgment of guilt of either suicide or murder. Was I wrong to thank God for the timing of her death?

The world was only two generations old when the first recorded murder occurred (Gen 4:8). The Biblical account of Abel's murder by his brother Cain reveals that Cain was filled with both envy and anger. His murder of his brother was planned and premeditated. The carnage that began with brother against brother in Cain's killing field continues today.

Sadly, with the expanded interpretation of the Sixth Commandment to exclude unintentional, accidental killing, we have arrived at a point where killing, violence, and violent behavior are accepted as being a part of life. Indifference to questions of life and death are so ingrained into the fabric of our society that we glamorize it in our media and entertainment.

One question that inevitably arises in discussions of the Sixth Commandment is whether God violated His own Commandment. Any answer to this question requires us to first determine whether God ever committed murder, i.e., without cause. God did kill people directly, and indirectly by ordering that people be killed. In the flood God saved Noah, his wife, and their sons and their wives. All the other inhabitants of the earth were judged as corrupted and perished in the flood (Gen 7:1). God ordered Joshua to kill every man, woman, and child in Canaan excepting Rahab, the harlot, and others in her house. Were all these people, including the children, judged to be evil? Yes. God told Moses that the Canaanites were wicked people, that they were always plotting evil. (Deut 18:9–12)

Other forms of killing that are outside the judgment of the Sixth Commandment are accidental killing, unintentional killing, capital punishment, just wars, and self defense. Each of these is addressed in the Bible. For certain offenses, constituted governments can impose the death penalty according to God's judgment (Gen 9:26; Rom 13:14). Killing in a just war does not constitute murder except when resulting from torture or atrocities (Rom 13:1-7). Killing resulting from self defense, e.g., home intrusions is not judged as murder.

In Matthew 5:22-23, Jesus taught, "You have heard that it was said of old, 'You shall not murder, and whoever murders will be liable to judgment.' But I say to you that everyone who is angry with his brother will be liable to judgment." Jesus expanded the definition of murder to include anger as murder in a spiritual sense.

Jesus also taught us to go far beyond simply avoiding murder. He warned us against harming another person by word or deed. He told us to treat even those who hate us with respect and to do all that is in our power to live in peace and harmony with them. To do this we must respect the God-given possession of human life.

45

PATIENCE

"You need to be patient, in order to do the will of God and receive what He promises." Heb 10:36. (GNB)

Rick made no effort to conceal his irritation for having to come to behavioral therapy. "This is not my idea and I do not want to be here. How long is it going to take? Let's get started"

His supervisor, who had directed the therapy, described Rick as a highly skilled, innovative design engineer who, unfortunately, had let his success go to his head. He gets upset when production questions his designs. He feels that he anticipates any questions production might have and there is no need for further discussion. His impulsive behavior has cost us competitively in a couple of cases. He is a good engineer, I would hate to let him go."

Not knowing how long Rick might stay in therapy, I took a direct approach. "Rick tell me about your relationship with production. Why do you get upset when they ask questions or offer suggestions? You need those people to make you look good."

His answers were predictable. I had heard the like before: judgmental, defensive, and self-serving. His words and his attitude paradoxically reminded me of a quote attributed to Adali Stevenson: "It's better to discuss a problem without solving it than to solve it without discussion."

Impatience is common to all of us. We want our needs satisfied quickly. We want instant fixes to all our problems, and detest long lines even as we wait for quick food. We want tomorrow today, and when things do not go our way, we get impatient. Patience is holding back immediate self-gratification for greater, more long-term outcomes. Patience is our willingness to wait until a more appropriate time for a greater promise of greater satisfaction.

Why is impatience, such as Rick's behavior. so offensive to God? Why did Jesus and Paul both condemn it? Why did Paul include patience as one of the fruits of the Spirit? A simple answer is that impatience is greed; it is selfish, it is putting our needs first, and it is unchristian It suggests that we want our needs satisfied at the expense of others. Impatience leads to competitiveness, which in turn can lead to conflict. The implied message of impatience is that I am more important than you—my needs are more critical than yours.

Simeon was a righteous, devout believer who had been told by the Holy Spirit that he would not die before he had seen the long-awaited Messiah (Lk 2:25-35). He was also a patient man; he waited for a promised event without any knowledge of when it might happen. All he could do was to wait and he did, patiently. In prayer. worship, and in humble and faithful expectation he waited, faithful to the promise of the Holy Spirit.

When Mary and Joseph brought their first-born son to the Temple for dedication to God, Simeon was waiting there, having been led by the Holy Spirit. After Jesus was dedicated in the Temple, Simeon saw Mary and Joseph. Taking the young Jesus in his arms, he burst out in song and praises to God.

Luke does not tell us how long Simeon had waited nor does he tell whether Simeon died soon after seeing the infant Jesus. What Luke does tell us is that Simeon waited patiently for an event without knowing when it would happen. He believed the promise of the Holy Spirit. He was a patient man.

No one is free of impatience, yet we see it more clearly in others than in ourselves. When confronted with feedback about our impatience, we tend to blame others and unfavorable circumstances. We argue that under more favorable circumstances, we would not have to be adamant to get things done our way. This is a weak argument. Impatience is a human attitude—it is not due to external circumstances. We can not go through life avoiding situations with unfavorable circumstances. Nor can we always change our environment to overcome our predisposition to impatience.

There is no easy cure for impatience. Even when we accept the necessity for change there is a lot of unlearning to do and relearning more appropriate behaviors. This process of change can be facilitated by prayer, psychotherapy, and growing older, and, hopefully, more wise.

46

PEACE

"Try to live in peace with everyone and seek to live a clean and holy life, for those who are not holy will not see the Lord." Heb 12:14. (NLT)

"Peace I leave with you; my peace I give to you. I do not give as the world gives. Do not let your hearts be troubled, and do not let them be afraid." Jn 14:27 (NRSV)

"Blessed are the peacemakers, for they will be called children of God." Mt 5:9 (NRSV)

Peace, like love, is a many splendored thing. We use the word many different ways; it has many different meanings. As a psychologist, I think of peace as a state of tranquility or freedom from disquieting or oppressive thoughts—the opposite of worry, anxiety, and doubt. As a military retiree, I still put a lot of hope in peace as the absence of armed conflict. As a former member of the American Arbitration Association I sought to resolve disputes between contending parties in a win-win fashion. As a neighbor I want to help others in any way that I can, especially in promoting harmony and good interpersonal relations—what Jesus might refer to as peacemaking. I use peace as a farewell when leaving a friend or concluding a telephone conversation. As a Christian, I seek peace of mind as a special gift from Jesus—the Prince of Peace.

All the uses of peace mentioned above, except the last, might leave the impression that peace is primarily a secular concern. Yet, the word peace appears in the New Testament over one hundred times, in all the New Testament books except 1 John. This widespread Biblical usage suggests a harmony between the sacred and the secular in their desires for peace. The critical difference surfaces when we consider how peace is sought or attained. In the secular domain, we tend to view peace as something we can obtain by our own design or efforts. When these efforts fail we unashamedly turn to Jesus because we have no other place to go. Jesus is the source and giver of peace. In John 14:27, Jesus promised, "Peace I leave with you, my peace I give unto you: not as the world giveth, give I unto you. Let not your heart be troubled, neither let it be afraid." Apart from our love of God and our faith in the authority and promises of Jesus, peace is an elusive goal, whether we seek it for ourselves or for others.

Christians are called to be peacemakers; it is a noble, divine calling; it is a rewarding (blessed) calling. Peace making—I also like the word peacekeeping—begins with a reconciliation with God. Peacemakers must themselves be at peace; they must be able to pray the words of the hymn, "Let there be peace on earth and let it begin with me." As peacemakers we are not contending for a Nobel Peace Prize, we are simply responding to God's call to work for peace—peace in our selves, our families, our churches, our communities, wherever the peace and tranquillity of God's people is disturbed, wherever love and harmony of God's people is disquieted. At the 1993 signing of the Israel-Palestine Declaration, Israeli Prime Minister Yitzhak Rabin declared, "Enough of blood and tears. Enough." What has gone wrong? It is now 2011 and blood is still flowing and tears are still being shed. Renewed efforts to bring the parties to the negotiating table make good reading, but our hopes continue to be shattered at the slightest provocation by either of the parties. Can/will they come to the negotiating table in good faith with other than a win-lose expectation? Can they find peace without fighting a war to get it?

Theologians, philosophers, and even politicians have long debated the issue of our basic nature, which in turn prompts the question of whether we really desire peace. Some see mankind as competitive by nature, others as cooperative. Some maintain that our basic nature is hostile and self-seeking; others see us as peace loving and kind. Which is it?

Having been made in God's likeness and image, we were once capable of living good lives, characterized by love and forgiveness. Since the Garden of Eden Fall, however, it has become increasingly difficult for us to avoid the twin sins of greed and idolatry and let our goodness come through. God wants us to live in peace and He made it possible for us to overcome every obstacle blocking our way. How? By putting our trust in Jesus Christ. Jesus is ready to give the peace of mind that we all seek. We can receive it whenever our troubled minds and souls cry out for it.

Peace.

47

PLEASING GOD

". . . . without faith it is impossible to please God, for whoever would approach Him must believe that He exists and that He rewards those who seek Him" Heb 11:6. (NRSV)

Pleasing others: is it a means or an end? Do we seek to please others because it genuinely pleases us, or do we seek to please others because we seek their favor and approval? Do we have a hard time saying "No" to the expectations and demands of others? Does our sense of well-being depend upon our being seen as a people-pleaser? Does our desire to please others mean that we have to displease ourselves? What is my motive or goal as I seek to please others?

These questions do not have easy, black-or-white answers. We want to say "It all depends" to each of them. These questions are difficult because they call our motives into question. Yes, I try to please others because I want to be seen as a friendly, easy-to-get-along-with person. It is not always easy. Some individuals tend to be inconsiderate, controlling, and demanding; they are takers, never givers. They are difficult to get along with. I try to be patient and understanding with them but sometimes it is more loving to avoid them. Ricky Nelson, in his song *Garden Party,* faced this problem. He sang all the familiar songs—he thought that's why they came. He lamented that since he could not please everybody at the party he had to please himself.

There have been a few persons in my life that I wanted to please, whatever the cost. My wife, my parents, my two children, my in-laws: these head the list. Not all my actions toward them were pleasing, but they were gracious in recognizing my intent and forgiving my mistakes. Through trial and error I learned what pleased them and always tried to act accordingly. The reward was always greater than the cost.

Today the single most important relationship in my life is with God, and my single most important goal is pleasing Him. The question of cost never enters my mind; I focus solely on the reward that He has promised. The Holy Spirit—my Counselor—is always ready and able to help me discern what is pleasing to God.

Careful never to trust my own judgment, I can gain access to the Holy Spirit through prayer.

Two preconditions to pleasing God are faith and intent. Hebrews 11:6 declares that without faith it is impossible to please God. We can have faith without good actions or, conversely, we can do good things without faith. God is more pleased with the former than the latter; faith is the *sine qua non*— the necessary condition. Without faith there is no way we can please God, what ever our intentions, whatever our actions. Hebrews provides an impressive list of persons who first believed and then sought to please God. There is Abel (v. 4), Noah (v. 7), Abraham (v 8.), and the list goes on including Job, David, Daniel, Moses, and Joseph, among others. But the most glorious instance of pleasing God was the life that Jesus Christ lived on earth (Matthew 3:17). What can we learn from these heros of the faith? First, there was an unfaltering, unquestioning faith that comes from the heart and, second, a compulsive desire to please God.

If we have that faith and that desire to please God we must confront the questions of how can we please Him. Is our desire so strong that we want to please God for His own sake, and not for some good that may come to us for pleasing Him? We can not avoid the end/

means question. I understand and accept the persuasion, it pleases me to please God, but I have to make pleasing God my supreme end.

Now the question is, "How do we please God?"

My late wife and I often discussed this question. She, typically, would begin with, "I have a simple faith," and then ask me if I could improve upon Micah 6:8.

"He has told you, O mortal, what is good; and what does the Lord require of you but to do justice, and love kindness, and walk humbly with your God?"

In a bit of one-up-man-ship, I would put on my intellectual cap and ask her, "What about love? What about the commandments to love God and to love our neighbor as ourself?" She would then play her trump card with the response, "Russ, whether we look at the Old Testament or the New Testament, God is the same. God told Micah what was pleasing; Jesus told us what is pleasing to God."

48

PRAYER

"This . . . . is how you should pray: 'Our father in heaven: May your holy name be honored; may your Kingdom come; may your will be done on earth as it is in heaven. Give us today the food we need. Forgive us the wrongs we have done, as we forgive the wrongs that others have done to us. Do not bring us to hard testing, but keep us safe from the Evil One.'" Mt. 6:9-13. *(GNB)*

"Pray at all times." 1 Thes 5:17. *(GNB)*

The most frequent complaint from my clients in therapy had to do with breakdowns in communication: with their spouse, with their boss, and, yes, with God. In all their complaints was the idea that their problems were caused by their inability to communicate effectively with significant others. They viewed poor communication as a villain; their troubled relationships were its victims. In my experience, paradoxically, I have found just the opposite to be true. Rather than being the cause of troubled relationships, communication is made the scapegoat for other problems in their relationships. This is especially true of our relationship with God. Our prayer life suffers unnecessarily when we feel separated from God, when we begin to wonder if God is listening. Strangely, at the very moment we most need to talk with God, we turn away with the excuse, "I don't feel like praying right now." Such is the nature of human nature.

Communication is the means of establishing and maintaining relationships with others. When relationships are good, communication tends to be both easy and rewarding. We usually have to make the initial effort to restore troubled relationships; we have to seek out the significant other. Maybe we call, email, or write a letter. It's different in our relationship with God. He is always calling to us; He is always taking the first step in restoring our relationship with Him. All we have to do is respond.

Of all the questions we can ask about prayer—what, when, where, how, why—the most significant is why.

What is prayer? That is an academic question, and the dictionary provides a variety of definitions. One definition I like that is not in the dictionary is that prayer is conversation with God. Prayer is not a monologue, but a dialogue involving both sharing and listening, both giving and receiving.

When should we pray? An off-the-top-of-our-head answer is, "Always." And that is what Paul told the believers in the church at Thessalonica (Thes 5:16) to do. To be always in prayer is not to spend sixty seconds of every minute of every hour of every day, etc., in prayer. Rather, we must develop an attitude of prayer; we must become prayerful people; we must make prayer the central dynamic of our relationship with God: morning and evening, special occasions, alone and in public worship. When ever. Where ever.

Where should we pray? In His Sermon on the Mountain, Jesus warned us against praying to the grandstands, suggesting that it would be better for us to pray in private. This was not a prohibition against public prayer. Rather, He was reminding us that prayer is a privileged, personal conversation with God. It is as natural for me to pray in the shower as it is for me to pray in my study. Wherever I am, I want to stay in touch with God: in my garden, in my greenhouse, before a client enters my office; before I start the engine of my car.

How should we pray? In front of me are books with the titles *How to Pray, The Essentials of Prayer,* and *How to Talk to God When You Aren't Feeling Religious.* Admittedly, these books can sensitize us to various components and dynamics of prayer. But they cannot tell us what is in our heart, what is on our mind, where we are hurting, or what we are feeling. Telling God about these things is the essence of prayer. These are the things God wants to hear. These are the things he wants to help us with.

Why should we pray? We pray to stay in touch. Lenora and I telephoned our daughter in Atlanta and our son in Raleigh because we loved them and wanted to share with them, and have them share with us. Our communication nourished our relationship, it reminded us of our interdependency; it brought us closer, and it made us human.

We pray to God to give thanks for his many splendid gifts, to learn his will for our lives, and to seek his forgiveness for putting our will before His. We pray for God's help with our problems, especially our problems with forgiveness.

Sometimes, when we called one of our children, we would get a busy signal or their answering service. It's a wonder of God's grace and power that no matter how many calls we make to Him, He can receive them all and, if we will stop talking long enough, talk back to us. The best answer to the question of why we should pray is found in trying to visualize what it would be like if we could not pray.

49

PRIDE

"I have told you this many times before, and I now repeat it with tears: there are many whose lives make them enemies of Christ's death on the cross. They are going to end up in hell, because their god is their bodily desires. They are proud of what they should be ashamed of, and they think only of things that belong to this world."
Phil 3:18-19. (GNB)

The English language, most people would agree, lacks the perfection and precision of mathematics. Two plus two always equals four, but words do not always mean what they seem. Although there are a few words which enjoy universally-accepted definitions, pride, unfortunately, is not one of them. It is a word we make do double duty. We make it a virtue when we speak of having pride in our work or appearance. It becomes a vice, however, when our pride mushrooms and joins conceit as opposite sides of the same coin. So ugly is pride as a vice that it leaves little room for pride as a virtue.

Grasping the essence of pride as something offensive to Christian morality is not easy. Dr. Karl Menninger (Whatever Became of Sin?, 1973) recognizes self-respect, self-approval, and self-confidence as favorable aspects of our normal self-concern. It is when our concern for self outweighs our concern for others that pride becomes a sin. Even when it is not considered serious enough to be called evil, Christians loathe pride because it distracts us from that which is grander. If we loathe pride in others it is easy to imagine God's feeling when He sees it in us.

Let's agree, for the purpose of this discussion, that there is both a good or fit pride and a bad or unfit pride. We can be proud that we acted rightly in a particular matter—that is a good or fit pride. We can boast that we alone could have acted as we did—that is a bad or unfit pride. The defining difference surfaces when we project the self as both the doer and beneficiary of the good action. Ironically, as we relish the experience of fit pride our desire for self-approbation blinds us to the danger signs of subjective or unfit pride. The trouble with pride is that so much of it is unfit that even a small amount of fit pride can lead to a lot of unfit pride.

Pride is considered by many theologians as being the original or base sin. It was pride (the sin of self-love) that tempted Adam and Eve to try to be like God. Pride was on the original list of seven deadly sins and remains so today. C. S. Lewis (*Mere Christianity*, 1943) describes pride as "The Great Sin." Other sins, he contends, " . . . are mere fleabites in comparison . . . . Pride leads to every other vice; it is the complete anti-God state of mind (p.109.)." Lewis would have agreed, most likely, that pride is the door through which all other sins enter into our lives.

How highly should we think of ourselves? Does showing concern and love for others mean we must first belittle ourselves? Answers to these questions fall into two conflicting extremes. Over and over again Jesus commended "the meek" and "the poor in spirit." And Paul (Rom 12:3) admonished us to not think more highly of ourselves than we ought to. But Jesus also taught that love and respect for the self were pre-conditions for loving God and our neighbors. We generally try to avoid people who show an inordinate, narcissistic love for themselves, just as we are discomforted by people who view themselves as more akin to animals than to God. We are called to reject unfit pride, first, because it is evil and, secondly, because it distracts us from the ultimate purpose of life. Struggling to always put the self first, defining all interpersonal relationships as competitive, and viewing life as a game of one-upmanship are never ending, pointless exercises in futility. Pride gets no pleasure from just being, doing, and having; it wants to be the greatest, do the best, and have the most. Focusing all our concern upon the self at the expense of others is a tragedy to God's family.

Being concerned for the welfare of others in the Christian sense of the word does not require everyone to become a Mother Teresa. It does suggest that we actively express our concern in helping, caring ways. The question confronting all of us is whether we invest our concern, energy, and resources in ourselves or in others. Claiming enough concern, energy, and resources for everybody—self and others—does not negate the self-or-others question. Our investments in others are most Christian when we experience some sense of sacrifice in our giving and our doing. It is only through caring for others outside or above the self that we experience fulfillment and a sense of belonging to God's family.

50

PROFANITY

"Since you are God's people, it is
not right that any matters of sexual
immorality or indecency or greed should
ever be mention ed among you. Nor is
it fitting for you to use language
which is obscene, profane, or vulgar."
Eph.5:3-4a. (GNB)

The news media recently reported three
instances of celebrity sports figures using
profanity when they disagreed with an official's
ruling. Apologies were made and dollar fines
were paid, but the fallout remains. Spectators
at these events were seemingly non-plussed.
Audiences at entertainment events have been
exposed to vulgarity and profanity to the
extent that they expect it even in expression
of the simplest ideas. Language that was once
considered crude and vulgar is now considered
acceptable, and the entertainment industry has
led the way in substituting vulgar expletives

for meaningful content. Sadly, media efforts to rate the appropriateness of movies, music, and videos have become so eroded they are no longer useful. Offending individuals dismiss their indiscretions by claiming that it was only words. "I didn't mean anything by it. Why does it bother you?" There are many men who would fight for the honor of their mother or wife's name, but do not hesitate to profane the name of God. Women are no less guilty. Who would argue the point that our society has become one of the most vulgar and profane in history? Surrounded by others who intentionally—with ease—use profanity leaves us with two choices: use it or risk being seen as an odd ball. Communication of the most simple ideas seemingly requires it. Sadly, we have to admit that most people have not been taught why bad language is bad (or even that it is bad). They have never tasted Ivory soap in their mouth. Why is profanity so commonly used today? An adequate answer to this question would require a lot of definitions and situational specifics. Still, we can make some useful conclusions, none of which justifies its use. Because profanity is capable of shocking listeners it is used to draw attention. Users want to demonstrate their macho qualities, their daring nature, their sense of liberation, and their rebellion by shocking speech and actions. Vying for attention is always competitive, causing users to try to out-do each other, leading to more course, vile, and irreverent language.

Another reason people use profanity is to compensate for their feelings of inadequacy in expressing themselves using conventional socially approved language. Profanity does not impress; it only shows contempt for others. It is the mainstay of lazy, contemptuous persons who feel they can enhance their position through use of profanity. Whenever interpersonal communication is laced with profanities any hope of honest, meaningful communication is destroyed.

I have not seen the movie *Apollo 13*, but was impressed by a reported interview with one of the crew members on that amazing flight. Commenting on the film, he said that it was for the most part accurate except that there was no antagonism between the crew members. He further said that they did not drink alcohol while in training, and no one on the crew used profanity. He was distressed that the film makers defended inclusion of profanity, arguing that it would add a note of reality, and energize and add flavor to the dialogue. (Note: 007, aka James Bond, was a man of action and he never used profanity.)

"Let the words of my mouth and the meditation of my heart be acceptable to you, O Lord, my Rock and my Redeemer."(Ps. 19:14).

What kind of words are acceptable to God? What kind of words does God reject? The Third Commandment (Gen 20:7)provides us one answer: we are forbidden to speak anything that so much as reflects irreverence toward God's name. But what is the test of the goodness of our words? Numerous Biblical preachments suggest that we should seek the guidance of the Holy Spirit in choosing all our words: words that are gentle, compassionate, and humble. These are the kinds of words that Jesus used; they were acceptable to God. Profanity can be described as any kind of words that God would reject. Could we impress God by using any words that fail this test? Would anyone dare to address prayers to God using words that were unacceptable to Him?

Individuals who defend their use of profanity by their freedom of speech, forget that they are still responsible for the words they use. They are also responsible for the effects their profane words have on others. A final consideration is this: the words we use show the kind of person we are. Profanity cheapens the user, leading to questions about their character. Individuals who are aware of the consequences of profanity seek to express their thoughts in words that are pleasing to God.

51

PRUDENCE

"Everyone who hears these words of mine and puts them into practice is like a wise man who built his house on a rock. The rain came down, the streams rose, and the winds blew and beat against that house but it did not fall, because it had its foundation on a rock." Mt. 7-24-25. (NIV)

The simplest definition of prudence is "knowing the right thing to do and then doing it." As simple as it appears, attempts to follow this definition in various real-world domains of decision making encounter all manner of intellectual and operational difficulties. First, how do we determine what is right? Do we mean morally/ethically right, or do we mean legally right, or do mean that decision that has the best chance of success? In seeking the right decision, do we take into account the costs and possible difficulties of implementing the decision? Does seeking the right decision mean that we have control over all the things that could go wrong? Does the problem we are facing have a single solution or we are having to choose from multiple possible solutions? To act prudently, we must be able to answer and consider each of the above questions.

A more complete definition of prudence would include the words cautious, practical, good judgment, wisdom, judicious, and discreet. The definition of each of these terms is virtually the same and each is defined in terms of the others. Still, there are differences between them, and the prudent decision maker—whether an individual or a group—should examine a proposed decision in terms of each of them. It must be realized, however, that the search for more and more information can easily lead us to fear making any decision. The virtue of prudence becomes a vice when we refrain from or unnecessarily delay making a decision when we are unsure of the outcome.

The above discussion supports a conclusion that the prudent decision maker is prudent in all things, even in those things in which he lacks expertise. Prudence is an attitude; it is a way of thinking and choosing, it is a character trait. Many, if not most of our individual decisions, are concerned with practical, everyday matters. The goal—

elusive as it is—is always to maximize the sought-after outcome. The word utilitarian (aka the business model) seems to fit. But what if the decision has consequences of value, justice, goodness, fairness, etc? How will others be affected by the decision? Prudence helps us to move along the continuum from a strictly utilitarian decision to a value-laden, socially responsible decision. Prudence, followed wisely and courageously, helps us to anticipate the moral goodness of a decision; it helps us to deliberate wisely and avoid rash, self-serving decisions.

It seems prudent at this point to ask, "How, or why, are our earthly, human decisions important to God?" The answer is simple. Prudence is not simply an intellectual or behavioral virtue; it is also a moral virtue. It is a moral virtue because decisions have consequences for persons beyond the decision maker. A prudent decision maker is, by definition, moral in his deliberations. Prudence and morality are synonymous. Prudent decisions makers always consider and promote the social good. God is a God of mercy, grace, goodness, and justice. God wants our interpersonal relationships to be characterized by these same virtues. We relate to others in terms of our perceptions and judgments about them, i.e., we make decisions about them and follow our judgments in relating to them. God had his prophet Micah (6:8) tell us what He expects of us in all our decision making and relating to each other: " . . . do justice, love kindness, and walk humbly with God."

In all matters of our faith and obedience to God's commandments the door to prudent decision making is spiritual discernment, which God gives in response to our prayers. All decisions have consequences and when these consequences affect others prudence dictates that we seek God's guidance.

52

PURITY

"My dear friends we are now God's children, but it is not yet clear what we shall become. But we know that when Christ appears, we shall be like Him, because we shall see Him as He really is. Everyone who has this hope in Christ keeps himself pure, just as Christ is pure." 1 Jn 3:2-3. (GNB)

Ivory soap is advertised as being 99 and 44/100 pure. No mention is made as to what the other 56/100 is. But we are left with the understanding that Ivory soap is not pure. One appropriate definition of purity is any matter that is unmixed with any other unlike substance. In the physical world few things are pure. Ivory soap is one of them. Our air is polluted, our water has impurities, and our food has substances we wish were not there. Virtually everything around us is a mixture. In order to have pure things, we have to spend time, energy, and money to get the foreign substances removed from the stuff we do want. (Enough of chemistry; it wasn't my best subject.)

Years ago, I was subpoenaed as a witness in a jury trial. I had to swear that I would tell the truth, the whole truth, and nothing but the truth. Wow! The court wanted my testimony to be pure. When I entered the United States Air Force, I took an oath that included the following words: " . . . I take this oath freely, without any mental reservation or purpose of evasion . . . ." The Air Force was concerned about the purity of my motivation. On a wall in my office I have a large framed print of a serene ocean scene. Looking toward the sea there are sand dunes and some seaweed vegetation up from the water's edge. It is inviting and calming. It appears untouched by humans, natural and undisturbed, except for a soda can lying in the sand. Why did the artist violate the purity of the scene with the drink can? My love-hate feelings toward the picture have left me without an answer to the question of "Why?"

The idea or standard of purity is necessarily accepted and widely practiced in the secular, physical realm. It is critical in the spiritual domain. It is, literally, a matter of eternal life or death. The word impurity appears in the Bible fifteen times but whatever the

context it speaks of the dire consequences
of impure thoughts, feelings, and behavior.
The word pure, by contrast, appears far fewer
tines but is always presented as one of the
ways we commend ourselves to God. (2 Cor
6:4-6). Purity is a positive virtue; it is
higher, grander state than simply avoiding
thinking or doing impure things. Purity is
more than the absence of impurity.

God forbids impurity; He commands purity.
Jesus taught the people about how important
purity is to God in His first sermon, saying,
"Blessed are the pure in heart, for they will
see God." (Mt 5:8) Obviously, the quality
of the heart is the focal issue in this
Beatitude. In the Bible, the word heart is
the seat or repository of all our thinking,
feelings, and doing. Today we use the word
mind.

Psychologists view thinking and feeling as
antecedents of behavior. Every impure action
is preceded by impure thinking. According to
Jesus (MT 12:334), Paul (Ph 4:8), and Proverbs
(23:7), purity is of utmost importance—it
is a cardinal virtue. Unfortunately, too
many persons engage in immoral, profane,
and blasphemous speech without thinking.
Such speech has become a way of life, being
constantly reinforced by public media. It
easily becomes habitual. James (3:8) describes
the tongue as "a restless evil and full of

deadly poison." My mother must have understood the danger of loose talk, since she always counseled me to count to ten before speaking. "People judge you by the way you talk," she reminded me.

Thinking and feeling are covert processes. They must be kept under control, else in unguarded moments they are expressed through overt behavior. Better than keeping impure thoughts under control, moreover, it is to not have them. It is not just impure behavior that God forbids, our private thinking and feeling are known to God and fall under His condemnation.

God is the absolute example of purity and to fellowship with Him we must be pure. God wants us near Him, but we cannot draw near carrying the baggage of impure thoughts, feelings, and behavior. Knowing the futility of our own efforts to cleanse ourselves of every impurity, God provided a solution. To Jesus God gave the authority and power to cleanse (forgive) us if we come to Him with repentance and sorrow, seeking His forgiveness. Jesus will give us a new, clean heart. Let us pray for diligence in keeping it clean.

53

REPENTANCE

"For God can use sorrow in our lives to help us to turn away from sin and seek salvation. We will never regret that kind ;of sorrow, But sorrow without repentance is the kind that results in death." 2 Cor 7:10. (NLT)

Given a choice, most people would choose not to talk or read about repentance—not even in the church. Sadly, repentance has a rather negative reputation. Perhaps it is because of misunderstandings about repentance: what it is, what is required, and why it is necessary. (It's also likely that repentance is resisted because it is understood.) Admitting our mistakes, recognizing our vulnerability to wrongdoing is never easy. It threatens our sense of well-being. We simply do not like looking into the mirror or, for that matter, letting someone else look closely at us. Much of the resistance to repentance is a result of faulty understanding of what is involved and why it is necessary.

As evidence of its importance, the word "repent," in its various forms, occurs more than 70 times in the Bible. It is an essential theme in the Scriptures. Repentance was the message of John the Baptist. The need for repentance was proclaimed by Jesus. It was the preachment of the Apostles on the first day of Pentecost. Throughout both the Old Testament and the New Testament, repentance is pictured as the first step in opening the door to God's forgiveness of our sins and wrongdoing.

What is repentance and why is it necessary? My answers to these questions are essentially theological, flavored by some psychological insights.

First, we must be confronted by our sin. The first of the Twelve Steps Program of Alcohol Anonymous is, "I am an alcoholic." In like manner, it is necessary for us to confess "I am a sinner." Next, we must evidence sorrow and remorse over our sins, both past and present. But simply confessing our sorrow does not go far enough; we must accept ownership of our sins without any thought of rationalizing or defending them. We must hate our sin and feel genuine shame and remorse.

With these steps behind us we must confess our sins, naming them one by one. We must also ask God to search our heart for sins we might have unconsciously committed. We must agree that our sins were wrong—that we violated God's commandments. Honesty of this type can be both scary and refreshing because we can see the joy of forgiveness that is awaiting us for our transgressions. Since we cannot be forgiven without repentance, we should want to repent as often as we sin. Rather than focus on the difficulties of repentance, let us look at it as a joyful experience. It makes it possible for us to know the joy of living a life pleasing to God. Further, repentance is necessary for personal happiness and emotional and spiritual growth. It is the only way we can free ourselves of the burden of guilt. Still, repentance is not a gloom-and-doom matter; it is a core part of God's good news for His children. It is a great blessing.

In the criminal justice system, wrongdoers are not required to repent. The purpose of our laws and the courts is to punish wrongdoers, believing that punishments will deter future transgressions. Neither is forgiveness offered if a wrongdoer should apologize and express sorrow. Punishment is viewed as the way wrongdoers pay their debt to society.

Repentance is more than being sorry for our sins. True repentance is a change of heart and a change of mind. The result is a changed life. Acts of repentance do not of themselves earn forgiveness. Rather, forgiveness is freely given by God, opening the door to reconciliation. We need never despair because we have sinned for as soon as we repent we are graciously received by God. Repentance dependably brings pardon and forgiveness.

Surprisingly, repentance is not something we do by ourselves; it is never purely our own doing; it is something that God does in us. We cannot repent and come back to God unless we are drawn to Him. No one can repent unless God grants repentance.

54

REVENGE

"You have heard that it was said,'An eye for an eye and a tooth for a tooth' but now I tell you, do not take revenge on someone who wrongs you. If someone slaps you on the right cheek, let him slap your left cheek, too." Mt 5:38-39. (GNB)

On January 16, 1919, the 18th Amendment to the U.S. Constitution was ratified. It prohibited the manufacture, sale, and transportation of alcohol. On December 5, 1933, the 21st Amendment was ratified. It repealed the 18th. What was previously prohibited was now authorized.

Unlike laws of man, God's laws do not change. And there is no Supreme Court to interpret the meaning of God's laws. God is the giver, the interpreter, and the enforcer of His laws. With these constraints in mind let's go outside the box to ask a hypothetical question. If you could be excused from having to comply with one of God's commandments or laws, what would you choose? I have asked this question in various ways of numerous persons in a variety of classroom and therapy settings. The most frequent response was revenge. Surprised? I was. I had expected adultery or, possibly, stealing would have been at the top of their list. I was surprised at their answers, but pleased with their logic. Respondents generally explained that being Biblically excused from the sins of adultery and stealing would not negate the fact that they were still morally and legally wrong. They did not see revenge as being morally or legally wrong to the extent that adultery and stealing were, and they also shared that they struggled to understand God's reasons for His rule against our seeking revenge when we have been wronged.

The respondents were more familiar with and understanding of the rule of "An eye for an eye" (Exodus 21:24) than with "'Vengeance is mine; I will repay', saith the Lord." (Romans 12:19). They questioned how we could have a just society if we did not punish wrong doers. Admittedly, revenge is a hotly contested cultural, ethical, and philosophical issue but, Biblically, there is no wiggle room between right and wrong behavior. Why does God reserve the right to vengeance? Because

He is the only being who can confront evil head on and remain unchanged. God is the only Being with love and grace sufficient to forgive and to pay the costs associated with His forgiveness

The rule of "an eye for an eye" was never meant to authorize or permit personal revenge taking. The intent was to authorize (even require) judicial punishment of wrong doers by what we today call the Courts. But this authorization was limited. The punishment had to be tempered with due process and fit the offense, it could not be greater. Any greater punishment was viewed as personal revenge and revenge is the property of God.

Personal revenge is driven by hate, fear, pride. anger, etc., and is contrary to God's law however we choose to defend it. Returning evil for evil only results in evil thriving.

Still, revenge has long been seen as a normal retaliatory response to aggression against us. "Don't get mad, get even." is often championed as a pattern of revenge behavior. "Tit for tat", too, is also defended as a justifiable reaction to disappointment, falsehoods, or hostility by others. Sometimes we feel so hurt that all we can think of is getting even. Punishing the offender is seen as the only way to even the score. Even though revenge is widely glorified in the media as the right thing to do, as Christians we must ask,

"Is it really the right thing?" Revenge is admittedly attractive and it is easy, but it is both morally wrong and un-Christian. And revenge can lead to legal actions against us. Revenge seekers report that revenge is sweet and they can point to some research findings which support their contentions. Whether we are merely considering taking revenge or actually acting it out, we can experience an initial glow or feeling of sweetness. But these finding are countered by other research which suggest that the initial surge of sweetness is momentary. The initial taste can be sweet but the aftertaste is bitter. What, then, can we do when we have been offended and feel the need for revenge? The best revenge is no revenge at all, especially when other strategies are available, e.g., forgiveness. In taking revenge, we are but even with the offender; in forgiving, we are superior. Forgiveness is given for the benefit of the offended, not the offender. And, contrary to arguments made by persons seeking justification for revenge, it is not necessary for the offender to apologize to be forgiven.

What would Jesus do? What did He tell us to do? Forgive our offenders and ask God to take over the vengeance part.

55

RIGHTEOUSNESS

"And he (Abraham) believed the Lord; and the Lord reckoned it to him as righteousness. (Gen 15:6) (NRSV)

"For we hold that a person is justified by faith apart from the work's prescribed by law." (Rom 3:28) (NRSV)

Suppose Judgment Day comes and we appear before the Judge. His first question is "Why should I let you into the kingdom?" How would we answer? If we replied, say, in the manner of the Pharisees that we had kept the Commandments, fasted twice a week, given a tenth of our income to the poor, etc., it would be easy for the Judge to point out the laws that we had not kept, sins that we had committed without knowing, for which we had not repented. Neither could we simply argue that we had lived a good life, hoping that we had a passing score. No, all we could do is plead for mercy, trusting God's grace for forgiveness of our sins through our faith in Jesus Christ. That faith is our only basis for salvation.

A basic doctrine of our Biblical heritage and therefore our Christian faith is that we are "justified" or declared "righteous" by God through our faith in Jesus Christ. This recognition raises two important questions. First, what is righteousness, and, second, how do we get it? For example, what is the source of righteousness and what do we have to do to be reckoned righteous? "Abraham believed God and it was reckoned to him as righteousness." (Gen 15:6).

Abraham did nothing more or less than believe in the promise of God. This tells us what we have to do to be declared righteous, i.e., believe. It also tells us the source of righteousness—it is given or imputed to us by God. Righteousness is a condition or state of being that makes us acceptable to God. It is based upon the character of God and is a gift of and from Himself. It is freely given by grace without conditions other than faith in Jesus Christ.

Is believing all that we have to do? The apostle Paul says, "Yes" (Rom 3:29). Paul's' preachment is that faith alone is the key to righteousness. He is strongly supported by Martin Luther, who translated Romans 3:28 as follows: "Therefore we conclude that a man is justified by faith alone without the deed of the law." Contrast this argument to James 2:14: "What good is it, my brothers and sisters, if you have faith but do not have works?" These counter arguments set forth two methods or paths of justification: justification by works, the legal or law method, and justification by faith, the gospel method. Both arguments have their adherents.

Paul addresses this dichotomy head on in Romans 2:13 by stating that if anyone does keep the law perfectly, he would receive eternal salvation as his reward. But, he quickly makes it clear that no one can fulfill the law's demands, for all are under the power of sin and lacking any sense of righteousness. Obedience to the law can result in many individual blessings, but fulfilling the letter of the law does not and cannot earn eternal salvation. The promise of eternal life is God's free and undeserved gift and is offered only through the righteousness of faith in Jesus Christ. God's righteousness cannot be earned by fulfilling the letter of the law. The law saves no one, Paul states, it only makes us aware of our sin.

Even though we cannot obtain righteousness by our behavior—doing good works—we are commanded to live Godly lives. Performing good works for God is not irrelevant. Wanting to serve God by ministering to others is an effect or result of righteousness, not the cause of it. Works are complementary to righteousness. When I joined my church, I promised to be faithful with my prayers, my presence, my gifts, my service, and my witness. Doing these things is not a substitute for my faith. Rather, it enriches my faith, it makes my faith more alive and vibrant. The reward is pleasing God; it is using His gifts to us in serving others, with joy and thanksgiving. Not doing these things calls the strength of my faith into question.

A strong, vibrant faith leads to good works, but it is not these works that will save us.

56

SELF-CONTROL

*". . . . when the Holy Spirit controls
our lives He will produce this kind of
fruit: joy, peace, patience, kindness,
goodness, faithfulness, gentleness, and
self-control. Here there is no conflict
with the law."* Gal 5:22-23. (NLT)

In Romans 7:14-15 Paul confessed to a
dilemma we all face. He admitted that although
he knew what was right and wanted to do the
right things he didn't always do it. To this
he added that he knew what was wrong and that
it was the last thing he wanted to do. Yet
somehow, he did it. The conflict that Paul was
facing is the most painful, excruciating kind
of personal conflict: it was internal.

To do or not to do was his question. A
person experiencing this kind of conflict is
at war with himself. With Paul, it described
a person who was trying to be good by his
own efforts but had not yet mastered the

temptation of satisfying the demands of his human nature.

Paul doesn't reveal what it is he doesn't want to do. but we can easily imagine Paul lamenting, "Why did I do that?" or "That was stupid of me." It's easy to identify with Paul because we have been there, we have faced the same temptations, we have experienced the same failure, we have made the same confession. Regardless of our personal situation or circumstances, we have faced the problem of how to control our behavior, i.e., to make our actual behavior conform to our desired behavior. This is the essence and purpose of control in all arenas of human endeavor, whether we are navigating a ship at sea, supervising a production line, or keeping a New Year's resolution to control our anger. Paul knew what was right and wanted to do it; he also knew what was wrong and wanted to avoid it. That was his goal. Perhaps Paul was too critical of himself, maybe he wanted to be perfect, forgetting for the moment that no one, other than Jesus, has lived a sinless life. Whatever, Paul was trying to avoid the bad and do the good by his own efforts. Romans 7 ends with his cry for help; Romans 8 tells the story of his deliverance.

"If Paul had to battle an inner conflict between doing good and avoiding bad what chance do we have?" we might ask. Paul's struggle against doing what he knew was wrong is an ongoing problem for all of us. Whether the temptations we face are minor or life controlling we all have them. The struggle against doing what is bad does not end when we become a Christian. Quite the contrary, the struggle can become more intense, more powerful. The reason is simply that we become more sensitive to wrong doing. Things we thought permissible to do before our conversion now bother our conscience. Things we thought "cool" now rob our sense of well-being. The bad in our lives can run the gambit from addiction to the internet to exploding with anger when things don't go our way. Whether the temptations we face are minor or major we are confronted with the continuing struggle between good and bad, between the flesh and the Spirit. This doesn't mean we might as well give up, that the struggle against wrong-doing is hopeless. We can find comfort in Corinthians 10:13: *"No temptation has seized you except what is common to man. And God is faithful, He will not let you be tempted beyond what you can bear. But when you are tempted, He will also provide a way so you can stand up to it."*

We can also find comfort in some recent research findings by Professor of Psychology Michael McCullough. After an extensive examination of a broad spectrum of relevant literature he concluded that religious people have more self-control than non-religious counterparts. He says that this is why religious people may be better at pursuing and achieving long-term goals and also might explain why religious people tend to have lower rates of substance abuse, better school achievement, less delinquency, better health, less depression, and longer lives. Two major conclusions drawn from his research are especially relevant to both our sacred and secular lives. First, religious rituals such as prayer and meditation affect the parts of the brain that are most important for self-regulation and self-control. Second, religious life—styles may contribute to self-control by providing people with clear standards for their behavior by causing them to monitor their own behavior more closely and by giving people the sense that God is watching their behavior.

Self-control is something that there just too little of. With self-control we can avoid the consequences of impulse buying, the harmful effects of overeating, and the burdens of a multitude of harmful addictions. Self-control saves us from social gaffes and loss of reputation. Self-control is a worthy goal throughout life.

How do we gain self-control? First, decide what it is about your life that you want to change. It can be something you want to move toward or something that you want to move away from. This is your goal. Pray for God's help; let God's spirit guide you. Discuss you goal of planned change with others-people who care about you and want to help you achieve you goal. It's easier to behave consistent with your goal when you know others are watching. Be patient, stay motivated, and put your past behind you. Failure in the past doesn't mean you won't succeed in your new effort. Walk humbly with God.

57

SELFISHNESS

"Where there is jealously and selfishness, there is also disorder and every kind of evil." Jas 3:16. (GNB)

Why do people act selfishly? Limited resources, say economists. Depravity, say philosophers. Egoism, say psychologists. Greed and gluttony, say theologians. What do you say? I asked my church school class for their opinions. Consider a sampling of their responses: Selfishness is a sign of weakness. Selfish people are haunted by fears of having to do without. Selfish people put their goals and priorities ahead of others. Selfish people suffer from unmet meeds. Selfish people suffer from a lack of moral development as children, and the list goes on. But do any of these examples satisfy our need to understand the causes and effects of selfishness? No. I like to answer this question with a question. As we go about our daily lives, involved in our daily activities and pursuits, whose well-being is being served, whose needs are being met? If our answer is "primarily mine" we are on the road to selfishness, if our answer is "exclusively mine," we have arrived. Hopefully, our answer is mutuality of interest.

The question of why we behave as we do defies easy answers. Aristotle and Socrates wrote about it as have other philosophers, psychologists, and theologians throughout the ages. The Apostle Paul wrestled with this question on a very personal basis (Romans 7:15). While our concern is understanding our "here and now" behavior and how we can guard against selfishness, we can enlarge our understanding by looking at some "there and then" examples of selfishness. Biblical history is replete with examples of selfish behavior. It began with Satan who was cast out of Heaven because of his selfish ambition to be equal with God. It was evident in the first generation as Adam and Eve sought to be like God. It was evident in the second generation as Cain denied being his brother's keeper. David's selfish pursuit of pleasure caused him to sin with Bathsheba. Count the number of times the words *I, me, mine, and myself* appear in Ecclesiastes 2:1-11. James and John selfishly sought the most prestigious positions in Jesus' Kingdom. The older brother of the prodigal son demonstrated a lack of love and understanding of both his father and his younger sibling. The variety of selfish behavior in the Bible and the motivation for it is easily parallelled in our contemporary society. We study the Biblical accounts, but do we learn from them? Admittedly, society is more complex and diverse today, and many questions about what is right and what is wrong are met with "it-all-depends" answers. So much so that someone has suggested we might as well learn to forgive since there is no cure for the sin of selfishness. Selfishness is seemingly viewed as a fact of every day life, and not an always unfavorable one at that.

Is selfishness an innate human behavior; are we hard wired to always act in our self interest or is it learned? If learned, what are the socio-cultural antecedents? Is it always negative? Can it be unlearned? What are the effects if it is allowed to go unchecked? Selfishness, like greed, lust, and gluttony, is typically considered a sin of excess, particularly when applied to material wealth. The key word here is excess, and I use it to describe persons who always want more of whatever brings them pleasure and a sense of well-being. These persons feel that giving away any part of their time, money, or effort would leave them with less. Growing up in a society that promotes self-interest by looking out for number one makes it hard to understand or appreciate the value of unselfish behavior, i.e. giving.

An individual or a society devoid of selfishness is hard to imagine. It is equally hard to imagine an individual or a society that does not benefit from what might be called enlightened self interest. It is well argued that always putting others first, to the exclusion of the self, means that the giver and the beneficiary are merely trading circumstances. An enlightened commitment to self interest hopefully means that individuals work to gain the means of helping others. This was the gist of Paul's exhortation to the church in Thessalonica (2 Thes 3:5–10). There is room in enlightened self interest for a genuine concern for the disadvantaged and the practice of old fashioned generosity.

John Wesley captured the essence of enlightened self-interest when he preached, "Earn all you can (author comment: without hurting others), save all you can, and give all you can."

58

SIN

"Jesus said to them, I am telling the truth: everyone who sins is a slave of sin." Jn 8:34b. (GNB)

In any discussion of sin we are immediately confronted by questions of definition. Its universal nature is clear; that we are all sinners is inarguable. But what is it?

Biblical definitions of sin range from a misstep or blunder to a failure to hit the mark, as in shooting at a target. The target in this definition is God's righteousness. Other definitions suggest it is a mean spirit, a disposition to behave in ways that have harmful consequences for God's family.

Included in this book are sixty-five of God's words of instruction, both prescriptions and proscriptions, both do's and don'ts. These instructions were given as part of God's plan for us to live righteous lives. If we fail to do what God has commanded we sin;

if we do what God has prohibited we sin. Sin is a generic word. We use it to refer to any unrighteous behavior. It is an umbrella concept, with all forbidden thoughts, words, and deeds included in its shadow.

Beyond the question of definition is the more difficult question of why we sin. And beyond the question of why is the matter of the consequences of our sins. Knowing the consequences of sinning makes the question of why we sin imperative. It invites a knee-jerk reaction but I am not suggesting that we sin in order to satisfy our selfish wants and desires, however wrong they may be. We do not sin for sin's sake alone. It is part of our conventional wisdom that any action that does not produce some desired outcome is a wasted action. This holds true for sin. Sin is a means, not an end. It is insufficient to say that sin is simply the absence of righteousness. No, we sin because we selfishly desire the rewards of sinning. We sin to get what we want rather than obey God's plan for our lives and receive what He has prepared for us.

A woman accused of adultery was brought to Jesus. It was customary, according to the Law of Moses, for her to be stoned to death. Asked for His opinion, Jesus replied, "Which of you has committed no sin may throw the first stone." All the accusers left silently.

Jesus neither judged nor prompted the woman's accusers, they knew they had sinned. They were convicted not for their sins but by their sins. They convicted themselves; they made no effort to explain or justify their sin.

As soon as Adam and Eve ate the forbidden fruit they became aware of their nakedness and because they were embarrassed they covered themselves, Their awareness of their wrongful behavior caused them to try to hide from God. They were convicted by their sin; their Garden of Eden was lost.

In a similar story, Zacchaeus, a rich, despised tax collector, encountered by Jesus, promised to give half of his belongings to the poor. The other half he would use to make restitution for wrongs he might have committed. He did this without any judgment or prompting by Jesus. In the holiness of Christ's presence, the unholiness of sin is evident. No one who is unholy can come into His presence and be in fellowship with Him. Zacchaeus wanted to be with Jesus, but realized that he had to make things right—to be cleansed through confession and repentance.

Sin—any sin—creates disharmony and separation in God's family. Our happiness, our sense of well-being, and our relationships with God and others all depend upon righteous living in thought, word, and deed. When we have secrets we cannot share with others, we separate ourselves from them. When we can not remember to whom we have told what lies we live in the shadows, always vulnerable to exposure. Whatever we gain by sinning (money, pleasure, etc.,) is always short lived; whatever we lose (reputation, integrity. etc.,)is always hard to recover. The husband who is unfaithful to his wife, as much as the business man who cheats on his partner, creates conditions that make a mutually satisfying relationship impossible. When we lie, cheat, deceive, or fail to show the concern specified by the Golden Rule, we separate ourselves from God and from others.

Are some sins more sinful than others? Is small-time stuff like padding expense accounts, breaking promises, and lying about our failings less serious than the red-handed, horrendous sins that make the daily headlines? Are some sins equated to misdemeanors while others are equated to felonies? Our everyday, run-of-the-mill faults—the sins no one can disown—hardly seem comparable to the flagrant crimes which cry to heaven for vengeance. And yet they are sins—all of them. What we must realize is that the more horrendous sins are possible only because the habit and nature of sinning was formed on a lower level of wrong doing. The sins of thought make possible the sins of word and deed, and the sins of one day lead to the soul-searching sins of a lifetime. We cannot harm ourselves, our neighbors, or society without, at the same time, sinning against God. Sin is an injury to God's Holiness itself. Holiness, which is in God, suffers when we act unjustly, deceitfully, or selfishly.

"I don't believe in God, why should I be judged by His rules? He can't make me live by His rules unless I agree, and I don't."

At first consideration this objection has an internal logic; it begs its own answer. And the questioner's sincerity makes it seem all the more plausible. My answer, without a moment of hesitation, is brief. Let us suppose you renounce your citizenship in the United States and become a citizen of another country. By choice, then, you would no longer be subject to the laws of the United States. But you cannot renounce your membership in God's family. He made you and He owns you; you are subject to His moral laws, and He will judge you. You have no choice in the matter. Your sin breaks your fellowship with God, but it does not remove your name from the roll of His family.

We cannot escape accountability for our sins, no matter how clever or elaborate our explanation or defense might be. We can neither hide from nor rationalize our sins. We can, however, escape the consequences of our sins by truly repenting and asking for God's forgiveness, which, in His grace, He is faithful to give.

59

A GREATER SIN

Jesus said to His disciples, "Things that make people fall into sin are bound to happen, but how terrible for the one who makes them happen! It would be better for him if a large millstone were tied around his neck and he were thrown into the sea than for him to cause one of these little ones to sin. So watch what you do." Lk 17:1-3. (GNB)

Posing nude for *Playboy* and playing the femme fatale role in the movie, *Basic Instinct,* earned Sharon Stone millions of dollars. It also earned her a "slutty and wild" public persona. Interviewed on ABC"s *20/20* (30Sep94) she dissociated herself from those roles. "I'm very, very monogamous and very shy. That's why I like playing some of those bigger-than-life characters . . . because, you know, there aren't any consequences."

No consequences? How can that be? Why was she paid huge sums of money if **Playboy** readers and theater goers were not receiving voyeuristic satisfaction from ogling her? If just one male lusted for her, if just one female wished to be like her, then there were harmful consequences. Both lust and coveting are sins, and causing others to lust and covet is a greater sin.

Most commentaries generally agree that Jesus used the phrase "little ones" to refer to not only young children but also to older persons who have not yet matured in their faith. It also seems reasonable to include here individuals who are easily persuaded by others, highly dependent people who are other-directed or outer-directed in their thinking and decision making. The dependence of children and our need to protect them from what is injurious, exploitative, and corrupting is universally recognized. But older people can be just as vulnerable and easily led astray. We must always try to be aware of the effect of our behavior upon other people, both young and old.

These circumstances justify our many laws designed to protect children. Consider the continuing complaints being made against Joe Camel, the suave advertising symbol. The underlying concern is that he has an inordinate influence in causing minors to break the law by buying and using tobacco products. In a similar manner, movies must be rated in terms of their suitability for children.

Contracts entered into by minors and incompetents are traditionally considered unenforceable because of their limited ability to understand and comply with the provisions of a contract.

In his letter to the Romans (2:12), Paul declares that the penalty for our sins is spiritual death. What Jesus is saying is that the penalty for causing or teaching another person to sin is even more terrible. The word picture of drowning in the deep sea with a millstone around our neck captures the utter horror of the penalty. Our passage ends with Jesus' admonition for us to be careful what we do. This is both stern and scary. It means, for example, that we can cause another to sin either actively or passively, either consciously or unconsciously. We can consciously, willfully introduce another person to drugs or illicit sex. We can unconsciously cause the same harmful effects by using or approving drugs and illicit sex.

We never know the effect of our behavior upon other people. During my college teaching career I often assumed a devil's advocate role in classroom discussions. My purpose was to stimulate students' thinking and help them clarify their positions and their value systems. I often cringed at the narrow line between helping and hurting students. Was I building them up or tearing them down? Was I helping them to become stronger and more resolute in their beliefs or was I leaving them confused and vulnerable? No wonder I always uttered a silent prayer before I went into the classroom.

Jesus' admonition to us to be careful what we do might, at first glance, seem unfair. "Why am I responsible for the sins of others, I have enough sins of my own.?" Aren't we trying to get everybody to be responsible for their own behavior?" Consider some of the excuses I have encountered in my counseling work:

"Sure, I use drugs. But you should see the neighborhood I live in." (The neighborhood is responsible.)

"Yes, I've abused my child. It's not my fault, I was abused, too." (The abuser's parents are responsible.)

"What's so bad about stepping out on my wife? I saw my father do it." (The errant husband's father is responsible.)

Who or what is responsible for these behaviors? When, or under what conditions, do we expect people to accept the responsibility for their own behavior? Can neighborhoods be blamed? Not all children from bad neighborhoods use drugs. Should parents be held accountable for the adult behavior of their children? Children of abusive parents have choices—they don't have to be like their parents. What would Jesus say about these examples?

Jesus is concerned that we do nothing to destroy the unity and harmony of his earthly family. If we went about teaching and encouraging people to sin against God's moral law, the effect would be disastrous. What Jesus wants us to do is to build people up, to support them, teach them God's way, and pray for them. As members of God's family we have a duty—a trust—to help people to do what is good and refrain from doing what is bad. We sin if we exercise a bad influence; we also sin if we fail to exercise a good influence when we should have.

60

STEWARDSHIP

"Each one, as a good manager of God's different gifts, must use for the good of others the special gift he has received from God." 1 Pet 4:10. (GNB)

As a child, I was aware that most of my friends had more than I did: better clothes, a bigger house, more toys, more spending money, etc. I wanted to improve the circumstances of my life; I wanted to be like the people on the other side of the tracks, where the grass was greener. Success, I knew, depended upon hard work, self-reliance, perseverance, delayed gratification, and playing by the rules of the game. I did not think of these values as being opposed to my religious values. It was simply a case of living in two different worlds, one secular and one spiritual.

Today, at age eighty-four, I consider myself as having crossed over the tracks. Unfortunately, I am often tempted to think that my changed circumstances are due to my own efforts and that my success is deserved. I planned well, worked hard, and sacrificed. I reasoned that others who have not succeeded to the extent that I have, were not as disciplined as I was, didn't have the dream that I had, and were not willing to work as hard as I was. Every time I start thinking this way, I hear God's voice:

"Russ, wouldn't you agree that I have been good to you through the years?"

"Yes, Lord, you have."

"Remember how I brought you out of your unpromising circumstances as a child? You were the first and only member of your family to get a college degree. I gave you Lenora and blessed you with children. You had a successful career as an Air Force officer, and after you received your Ph.D. you enjoyed another fulfilling career as a college professor. Your health is good and you have prospered."

"Yes, Lord, you have been good to me, and I'm thankful."

"Russ, what have you done for Me lately?"

Conversations with God can be sobering, especially when He asks hard questions. Can I boast of what I have accomplished? No! I know that God has blessed me. What God is asking of me is that I be a good steward of what He has given to me.

In Biblical times, a person who cared for another's property was called a steward. Implied in this historical usage of the word is the special trust that characterized the relationship between the owner of the property and the steward to whom it was entrusted.

The church has resurrected the word stewardship from a lowly, demeaned status and elevated it to a role of spiritual significance. Aside from its current secular usage to designate positions of trust in such fields as transportation (ship's steward), hospitality (hotel steward), and labor unions (shop steward), the word steward is used almost exclusively by the church. It is used, for example, to refer to people entrusted with the church's administration and ministry. It has gained extra prominence by its use in referring to all people as being stewards of the gifts and graces given to us by God.

Also, a part of the legacy of the word steward is the idea and practice of the tithe. Throughout both the Old Testament and the New Testament there are teachings that the tithe is our obligation to God. It is our obligation because everything we have really belongs to God. We do not own anything at all, not even the clothing we wear. Everything we call our own has been entrusted to us by God, Who owns the universe and everything in it.

The word tithe has unfortunately taken a narrow meaning because of its being equated to a tenth of our earnings. It is a measure of our stewardship when we regularly give a tenth of our income to God. But when we take refuge in the limits of the tithe, when we could have easily given more, our giving becomes legalistic. We give only what the tithe requires. It is much like paying our taxes—we don't want to pay any more than we have to.

The Book of Genesis tells how God gave us dominion over all that He had created. His willingness to entrust His creation to us implied a staggering responsibility for stewardship, one we have not performed well. We have destroyed, polluted, wasted, hoarded, and otherwise diverted the resources of the earth to unholy purposes. We have been poor stewards.

Stewardship is more that safeguarding or caring for God's gifts to us. Jesus made it plain in his parable about the gold coins (Mt. 25;14-30) that we are expected to develop our gifts and use them in serving others. God wants us to be His hands, His feet, and His voice in doing good things for others. Stewardship is about what we do with what we have been given.

61

THIEVERY

"Do not steal." Ex 20:15. (NLT)

Imagine a world where we did not have to use locks, surveillance cameras, electronic security systems, or build prisons to house violators of the Eighth Commandment—a world where such words as bribery, cheating, extortion, fraud, pick pocketing, plagiarism, and shoplifting were infrequently used—a world where private property was respected. "Will never happen, it's unreal, contrary to human nature," you might argue. Admittedly, the daily police blotter does seem to support you. From Wall street to main street, there are continuous revelations of financial shenanigans, house break ins, shop lifting, and other acts of unauthorized taking. Wrong doers seemingly no longer feel any remorse or sense of guilt even when they are caught—shame, perhaps, but not guilt. One would think that the Eighth Commandment has been replaced by the Eleventh: Don't Get Caught.

From the beginning of Biblical history, stealing has been a problem (Exodus 20:15), and it is a problem today. Stealing is the unauthorized taking of something that belongs to another. It does not matter what is taken or the reason given for taking it, or from whom it is taken, the act of taking is thievery. Why do people steal? Let's look first at the case of kleptomania, which can be described as compulsive or pathological stealing. Kleptomaniacs can not resist the temptation to steal. The act of stealing—not the specific object taken—is their goal. Beyond kleptomania, there is a wide gambit of proffered reasons ranging from need to revenge to thrill seeking. Contrary to popular opinion, stealing is seldom done for purely economic or need reasons. Some takers do point to need as their reason for stealing, thinking it justifies the taking. Other takers explain simply that it is easier and quicker than working. Combining this line of reasoning with the low probability of getting caught actually strengthens their temptation to steal. Even less constraint is felt when they take from Wal Mart, compared to taking from a neighbor.

Pushing aside kleptomania and all the ingenious excuses and reasoning offered by violators, greed and covetousness are the main reasons for stealing. This is equally true of the person taking a one—dollar object from Wal-Mart and the person who defrauds investors of millions of their life savings through some clever scheme. I was recently told of a British priest who advised his congregation that it was acceptable to shoplift from large supermarkets since the cost is ultimately passed down to consumers in form of higher prices. Imagine that. What would Jesus say? Stealing is wrong; it is never right. Why? Because the law of Christ condemns it. (Ephesians 4:28)

Burning a copy of a copyrighted CD to give to a friend is stealing. Giving less than a fair day's work for a fair day's pay is stealing, as is the obverse. Consciously incurring huge debts before declaring bankruptcy is stealing. Plagiarism, using another persons's literary works without giving credit, is stealing. And the list goes on to include padding expense accounts and making false deductions on tax returns. Let me make the case that the worst kind of stealing is from God. When I was received into the local congregation of my church, I vowed to uphold the church with my prayers, my presence, my gifts, my service, and my witness. If I withhold or give less than I am able, I am stealing—robbing from God. See Malachi 3:8-9.

The cadets at the Air Force Academy agree to live under an Honor Code that requires "We will not lie, steal, or cheat . . . ." Violations of the Code were rare; the advantages of living and teaching in that environment were many. It was a way of life; everyone, both cadets and staff, benefitted. God desires that His people on earth create and observe that same way of life. The Greatest Commandment—the Love Commandment—(Matthew 22:37-40) can point the way. If we love God, we would not steal from Him. If we love our neighbor, we would not steal from him.

62

TEMPTATION

"Keep watch and pray you will not fall into temptation. The spirit is willing but the flesh is weak." Mk.14:38b. (GNB)

Temptation is the word we use to describe the lures and enticements to violate a promise, trust, value, goal, etc., for the expectation of personal gain in the form of money, power, fame, or pleasure. Although athletes are tempted to train less diligently and dieters are tempted to sneak another chocolate, temptation is primarily a religious concept. In this sense, only people who have chosen to follow Christ—to do what is good, righteous, and pleasing to Him—can be tempted.

Becoming a successful athlete, dieter, or Christian is a continuing struggle, requiring commitment, discipline, and sacrifice. For the Christian, it is a struggle between good and evil, between right and wrong. It is a conflict between knowing and doing God's will and what we want to do—following our own will. It is a conflict between the demands of our natural selves and our transformed, born-again selves. There are no blanket immunities from temptation; we all have weak spots and weak moments which plague us constantly. For one person, it might be a foul temper or lying; for another it might be impure thoughts or forbidden sexual behavior. Whatever, the fault is always with the tempted, not the tempter. (See Luke 17:1-3 for the punishment God visits upon people who cause little ones to do wrong.)

Situations can present opportunities for us to do wrong, but temptation arises from within. When we try to blame others for our failings, as Adam did with Eve, we are really saying that it was not our fault. Blame the tempter, not the tempted, is our argument. If we are weak and realize that certain situations and circumstances are too attractive for us to resist, avoid those situations. A successful Wall Street broker was sent to prison for cheating his clients. He later explained, "Yes, we had a code of ethics we tried to follow but working in such a heady, exciting environment was too tempting. For me, it was a case of greed gone awry."

Whatever we gain by surrendering to temptation (money, pleasure, advantage, etc.,) is usually short-lived; whatever we lose (integrity, self-esteem. etc.,) is hard to recover. When we lie, deceive, divulge a confidence, or fail to show the concern specified by the Golden Rule we sin against both God and others. When we can not remember to whom we told what lie we live in the shadows, always vulnerable to exposure. When we have secrets we cannot share with our children we isolate ourselves from them.

Since God is holy He cannot be tempted to do evil; since Satan is evil he cannot be tempted to do good. There is no debate on God's part about doing evil; there is no debate on Satan's part about doing good. The closer we come to either God or Satan, the less conflict we will experience—the less we will be tempted. We can not be tempted to sin if we are already possessed by it. If we are on the bottom floor we can not fall down the stairs. On the other hand, even after we have turned from sin, we are often tempted to serve our natural desires to the detriment of our spiritual needs.

When tempted, we are prone to say, "God is testing me." But James (1:12-15) reminds us that God cannot be tempted by evil nor does He tempt anyone. Each of us is tempted by our own desires. When we give in to temptation, we sin. When our sin becomes full blown and possesses us, it gives birth to our spiritual death.

Surprisingly, temptation can have a beneficial effect. I say can, because it depends upon how we respond to it. Three paths or responses are available to us. Whichever path we follow, we are being tested. First, we can indulge our temptation arguing that the only way we can know our impulses is to act them out. In the process we still feel compelled to offer all kinds of excuses and rationalizations in order to assuage our guilt and hoodwink those who know about our behavior. A second path involves trying to repress the impulse or temptation into our unconscious mind. This path distorts reality; it is dishonest. It requires a lot of effort and attention and offers only minimal protection against the resisted impulses. Denying we have evil impulses does not mean they are not present in our heart. Try as we may, there is always the possibility that in an unguarded moment they will reappear.

The third approach is the honest approach. It requires an admission that we are being tempted. Only by admitting and accepting the presence of temptation in our life can we do something about it. As long as we deny its existence, we can do nothing about it. Even then we can do little on our own to successfully suppress the evil impulses that besiege us. Two things are required: honesty and prayer. "Dear God, this temptation is attractive, and it will not go away. I'm frightened by my weakness. I don't want to displease you. Enlighten me to know your will for me, strengthen me to do your will. Thank you Lord. Amen."

God lets us be tempted but it is His aim and purpose to keep us from falling. When we successfully resist temptation we are made stronger; our character is strengthened, and we start living on a higher plane. God is pleased.

63

A TREE AND ITS FRUIT

"A healthy tree does not bear bad fruit, nor does a poor tree bear good fruit. Every tree is known by the fruit it bears; you do not pick figs from thorn bushes or gather grapes from bramble bushes." Lk:6:43-44. (GNB)

Jesus' analogy comparing fruit trees and Christian fruitfulness is not lost on horticulturists and anyone who grew up on a farm, as I was. Growers of fruit plant good, high quality trees because they want to harvest good fruit; when a tree produces good fruit the grower reasons that he has a good, high-quality tree. Sometimes, what is supposed to be a good tree fails to produce good fruit. Improper grafting and poor pollination are possible reasons for failure. Sometimes, too, undesirable bushes find their way into the orchard or garden. They occupy space, consume moisture and fertilizer, and produce only thorns and brambles. Serious fruit growers remove them.

Early in life, I developed a love affair with trees that continues to this day: all kinds, but especially those that produce delicious fruit and berries and those that provide beauty and shade from the Georgia sun. Knowing my feelings about trees, my second grade teacher introduced me to Joyce Kilmer's poem *Trees*. The lines describing how "a tree looks at God all day and lifts it's leafy arms to pray" helped me to both praise God and give thanks for His joyous creations. Today, I enjoy twenty-one varieties of fruit and ornamental trees planted in the expanse of my lawn. There is a story and a memory associated with the planting of each tree— always planted to the glory of God to be enjoyed and appreciated.

I do not know God's purpose for thorn and bramble bushes. Maybe they help us to appreciate the good trees that produce good fruit. Every tree has its purpose; it is hardwired to produce its particular fruit in season—it cannot do otherwise. In a like manner, every human life is created and sent into this world for the purpose of producing good fruit—to add to the threshold of goodness in God' world. Unlike His plan for His trees, God gave us—His children—free will. We can and often do act contrary to His expectations; we do not produce good fruit. Missing the mark of producing good fruit, we dishonor God.

Spiritually speaking, what is good fruit and how do we produce it? First of all, it is more than the absence of bad fruit; it is more than well-intentioned activities. It is hard for us to move past the idea that we have to work (perform) to gain God's favor, to please God. Abraham was caught in this trap of erroneous thinking until God explained to him that the path to righteousness began with faith, not good works. Doing good deeds can gain us the approval of our neighbor but unless our good deeds are done for the glory of God they are empty as far as gaining God's favor. Abraham was declared righteous because of his faith. He let the Holy Spirit guide him on a journey to a distant land that he had never seen before.

Producing good fruit is more than following a compilation of prescriptive rules. I earned a Boy Scout badge by "helping little old ladies across the street." While the ladies appreciated my help, I have to admit that my goal was to gain the badge. I can not remember whether, after I received my badge, I ever helped anyone else across the street. Producing good fruit is more than a one-act play; it is an ongoing journey that we choose to follow, led by the Holy Spirit. Before we embark on our journey, however, we have to reckon with two preconditions: love and faith. Is my love for God so great that I am willing to serve Him, and Him only? Am I willing to trust God—that He will not desert me on the journey; that He will not ask me to do anything or go anywhere without preparing me for the task? Abraham and David were willing; both were declared friends of God.

Fruitfulness is a very elusive concept—hard to put our fingers on it. Like the wag said, "I can't define it but I know it when I see it." The safest, most certain way for us to bear good fruit is to let God define it for us. Praying "Thy will be done," we should pray for the Holy Spirit to guide every step of our journey to fruitfulness and righteousness.

64

WORK

"I appeal to you to be shepherds of the flock that God gave you and take care of it willingly, as God wants you to, and not unwillingly. Do your work, not for mere pay. but from a real desire to serve." 1 Pet 5:1b-2. (GNB)

A famous quote attributed to Sigmund Freud states that all in life is *Leiben und arbiten* (love and work). For Freud, the freedom to derive satisfaction from both love and work is a core characteristic of a psychologically healthy person. Our capacity to love, for example, is influenced by the self-esteem we receive from work. In a like manner, our ability and our motivation to work—to produce, to serve—is influenced by the quality of our love relationships.

Christianity has buttressed this belief with its view that work is done out of our love and concern for all members of God's family. Work is the means of earning one's living so that we do not have to beg or become a ward of the state. By work, too, we earn money so we can provide for the poor.

Making distinctions between "work" and "job" seems helpful at this point. Job is more closely related with the things we do for financial reward. In contrast to the idea of job is the grander concept of work which has the flavor of mission or calling in a persons's life. Work is the activity that mature people pursue with a sense of meaning and worth. Although not everyone needs a job, everyone should have the goal of work.

There is an often-told story of a cobbler who boasted, "My business is saving souls. I repair shoes (soles) to pay for the expense of saving souls." He saw saving souls as his work (an end); repairing shoes as his job (the means). That is an unfortunate view. When he strives to repair every shoe to the best of his ability, his secular job takes on a spiritual purpose.

Admittedly, most of us have to work for a living; this is the purpose of a job. Without wealth we have no choice aside from accepting welfare. But when we do something because we have to, we never give it our best effort; we do just enough to get by, and having this value system invites shoddiness and irresponsibility. We do have a choice, however, in how we feel about our job, especially when it creates goods and services valued by society. We can work because we want to, giving the job our best. When this happens we are working for both economic and moral reasons. This is the spirit of willingness that Peter admonishes us to show.

Throughout the Bible we can see work as an integral part of God's plan for us. God is often pictured as one who labors: a vine dresser (Ezek 15:6), a pottery maker (Gen 2:7), and a soldier (Isa 27:1). Jesus was a carpenter (Mk 6:3), and Paul was a tent maker (Acts 18:2). The disciples—all working men—were mostly fishermen. While the gospels caution us against an excessive or exclusive concern with job and the things of this world (Mat 6:24), they also make clear that work is a serious responsibility of the Christian (Lk 12:41-49).

Western society—the parent of the work ethic, sometimes called the Protestant work ethic—has traditionally cherished work and the related values of self-control, sobriety, and perseverance. Work not only pleases God, it also satisfies the deeper yearnings of the human spirit. Economically, work brings financial rewards, spiritually and psychologically, it provides a sense of purpose and self-worth. Work, thus, is a measure of creatively expressing what is important in our lives. It is something mature people want to do—more importantly, it is something they must do.

As workers we are responsible to use well all that God has entrusted to us. Land, energy, money, time, materials, and services: all these are necessary for us to produce the goods and services needed and desired by society. We must use them well. To squander, waste, or misuse any of these resources results in lowered levels of needs satisfaction for God's people. How we work and how we feel about our work makes the difference between mediocrity and excellence.

Why, we might ask, is the question of how we feel about our work and how we perform our work important to God? It is because the opposite of work (the absence of work) is laziness, inaction, indifference, and lack of concern. The age-old word for this human condition is sloth, which has come down to us as one of the seven deadly sins. It is deadly because of its negative consequences for God's family. When we fail to give our best at work, we are guilty of stealing from our employer. When we accept good money for bad work, we are guilty of benefiting at the expense of others. When we work at jobs which lack social legitimacy (adult book store, gambling casino, etc.), we are diverting our skills and gifts to activities which vilify God and corrupt His will for us. When we lose our sense of honesty and fidelity in our work, we lose our sense of God's presence in our lives. Both the work we do and the spirit in which we do it should glorify God.

65

WORRY

"Don't worry about anything, but in all your prayers ask God for what you need, always asking Him with a thankful heart. And God's peace, which is far beyond human understanding, will keep your hearts and minds safe in union with Christ Jesus."
Phil 4:6-7. (GNB)

Of all our human capabilities, the ability to feel is the most baffling. Human emotions can and do run the gamut from positive to negative—from desirable to undesirable. We relish positive feelings such as joy, happiness, etc., and generally try to maximize them. At the same time, we try to avoid negative feelings such as anxiety, fear, etc.

All our emotions—both positive and negative—were given by God as parts of a single package. We cannot be choosy, accepting positive emotions and rejecting negative ones. Pursuing positive emotions to the exclusion of negative ones tends to narrow our perceptual field about the presence of and approach to our problems. Efforts to diminish negative feelings have the unintended effect of reducing our ability to feel anything at all.

Conventional wisdom suggests two things we should never worry about. They are things that never happen and things that have already happened and cannot be changed. Still, worry is so common that it is tempting to ask whether it serves any useful purpose. Although worry is bad, is it all bad? Mark Twain realized this when he said, "I'm an old man and I've faced many problems in my life, most of which never happened." Although it is more often negative, worry can be constructive if it alerts us to the fact that something is wrong in our lives and prompts us to action—if it helps us to start thinking about how to cope. Worry is useful only if it prompts us to action; all other worry is pointless.

"Don't worry", is an idea that is as old as the Bible. King David, who had lots to worry about, said, "Do not fret because of evildoers." Jesus admonished his disciples, "Let not your heart be troubled." The Apostle Paul wrote, "Be anxious for nothing . . . ." Matthew wrote, Don't worry about tomorrow . . . each day has troubles of its own." All these preachments can be summed up as a command of God's word, "Don't worry, pray about everything, worry about nothing."

Despite all the sound theological/scriptural reasons not to worry, people still carry around an unnecessary load of anxiety and fear. Do we sin when we worry? Is worry an insult to God? Can worry so completely hijack our mind that we trust our own abilities rather than trust God? My answer to each of these three questions is yes. The scriptural evidence is self-evident and inarguable. Let's also look at the psychological evidence. Worry can alter our thinking. It perpetuates itself—we become what we think about. Faulty thought processes result in faulty decisions about the problems we face. Worry affects our behavior, causing us to do things less confidently, and less effectively.

Let's also look at the physiological evidence. A leading therapist at the famed Mayo Clinic once said, "Worry affects the circulation system of the body—the heart, the glands, the whole nervous system. I have never known a man who died because of overwork, but many who died from worry."

Since worry stems from a feeling of helplessness, the best insurance against it is to demonstrate our faith in God and recognize our dependence upon Him. It is precisely the fear of adverse happenings that are beyond our control and causes us to worry about their consequences. Worry replaces our trust and dependence on God. Certainly, we need to pay attention to the problems we face in life, but Jesus urges us to stop worrying about our problems to the extent that they dominate our thinking, feeling, and behavior. We can not worry and serve God at the same time (Mat 6:24). We need to redirect the focus of our lives onto God's Kingdom and His righteousness. That requires us to live by God's words and put Him first in our lives. Begin by praying the Serenity Prayer each day. It works.

God grant me the serenity to accept the things I cannot change, the courage to change the things I can, and the wisdom to know the difference.

CPSIA information can be obtained
at www.ICGtesting.com
Printed in the USA
LVHW040442060922
727646LV00016B/93